# DON'T DIE BROKE!

# DON'T DIE BROKE!

*A Guide to Secure Retirement*

**New Edition,
Completely Revised
and Updated**

## MELVIN JAY SWARTZ

*A Dutton Paperback*

E. P. Dutton    New York

For information contact: E.P. Dutton, 2 Park Avenue,
New York, N.Y. 10016

Library of Congress Cataloging in Publication Data

Swartz, Melvin Jay.
    Don't die broke.

    1. Aged-Legal status, laws, etc.—United
States.   2. Estate planning—United States.
3. Old age pensions—United States.   I. Title.
KF390.A4S9   1978      340'.02'40565      77-27564

ISBN: 0-525-47499-4

Published simultaneously in Canada by Clarke, Irwin & Company Limited, Toronto and Vancouver

10 9 8 7 6 5 4 3 2

Second Edition

MELVIN JAY SWARTZ is a practicing attorney in a retirement community. His law firm deals with the areas of estate planning, probate, and the legal problems of the aged. A graduate of Boston University School of Law, he has counseled more than 4,000 retired people in Sun City and Scottsdale, Arizona, and lectures frequently around the country on the subjects in this book.

# CONTENTS

# INTRODUCTION: MAKE YOUR RETIREMENT ENJOYABLE

A large number of retired and widowed people are in serious distress. They are annoyed, hounded, abused, and depressed. A surprising number live in fear. Anxiety about the future exposes them to profiteers and prevents them from seeking valid solutions to their problems. But you can avoid this unnecessary situation and make your retirement enjoyable.

Careful planning and prudent management can minimize the traumas that retirement often brings, but the responsibility for protecting yourself is strictly yours. The realtors, mutual fund salespeople, annuity peddlers, and bank employees who act beyond the scope of their expertise cannot help but mislead you. Do not seek or take technical advice from just anyone, just because it is "free." Enormous profits motivate the unscrupulous who offer this ultimately very expensive advice.

This is the first time in modern history that most people can anticipate retirement. Prior to 1937 retirement was only possible for the well-to-do. The Social Security system and the increase in pension and profit-sharing plans now make it possible for the average person to consider retirement. You are, therefore, a member of the first "retired generation" and a part of a grand experiment.

Many mistakes were made in the general planning for mass retirements. This was to be expected. As time passes pension and profit-sharing plans will be improved so that the average working person will not have to give up so much of his or her pension payments and take a substantially reduced monthly check in order to guarantee that modest monthly payments continue for a surviving spouse. It is hoped that in the future pension and profit-sharing plans will have a cost-of-living increase built in and will be guaranteed by federal insurance so that they will not disappear if a company goes bankrupt. Retirement communities will be better planned. Society will find ways to use the tremendous talents gained by the retired in a lifetime of work experience. We all hope and expect that retirement in the future will become more valuable to society and more enjoyable for the individual. But this does not excuse us from the responsibility of making the best of what we have today.

This book is a guide for the widowed and retired. It explains wills, trusts, probate (when to avoid it and when not to), joint tenancy, and taxes. It discusses ways to protect your assets, what to do when a spouse dies, and how to avoid legal problems in a second marriage. It provides criteria for making decisions. Because necessity demands that such decisions be based on certain principles, the advice of competent counsel should be sought on the particular application of these principles to your personal needs. This book is designed to help you understand what options are available to you before and after retirement so that you can avoid mistakes and recognize your need for professional advice.

The scope of this book is therefore limited. It does not deal directly with the psychological, social, and emotional problems of retirement, but the advice it offers for understanding and dealing with legal and financial problems can help alleviate the anxieties that may be caused by lack of understanding of legal and financial intricacies.

Your most common problems with Social Security will be discussed briefly here. More detailed information is available without charge from your local Social Security office, which is staffed by competent, helpful employees who will be happy to assist you with any Social Security problems.

I do not presume that the average person delights in reading lawyer-like discussions; therefore, lay language is used throughout this text whenever possible. If legal terms are necessary, they are explained in clear, simple language.

This revised edition of *Don't Die Broke!* was prepared subsequent to the Tax Reform Act of 1976. This law made substantial changes in income taxes, capital-gains taxes, estate taxes, and gift taxes. The particular taxes are not discussed in detail, although reference is made to them. You should seek your own independent counsel to determine what your individual estate-tax consequences will be.

This book will be of service to those who have minimal assets, and cannot afford to lose any of what they have. It will also help those who have substantial assets, for it will show them how to preserve what they own and perhaps increase their estates. The common problems that all retired people face are analyzed and reasonable solutions suggested.

I hope this book will help readers to minimize legal fees, bank commissions, estate expenses, and taxes after death. Most of all, I hope they will learn how to maximize their incomes during retirement and not lose their assets while they live.

Every retired person can benefit from one piece of advice: *Don't try to get something for nothing*. Free advice is often useless; cheap advice often backfires. You cannot afford to lose your assets, but you can stop worrying about your future. Protect yourself, and your future will be secured.

# PART ONE:

# *Before You Retire*

# 1. PLAN FOR
# RETIREMENT

You owe it to yourself to enjoy your retirement. You can anticipate many good years beyond your early sixties and new ideas and new concepts are awaiting you. No one has to be a stick-in-the-mud. No one has to run out of money either. You can keep what you have and perhaps increase your assets, but only if you plan carefully and seek independent, prudent, professional advice in planning for retirement, choosing the option that will give you the maximum benefit from your pension plan, and managing your postretirement assets. You do not have to make the same mistakes as your predecessors and blindly follow the advice of bank clerks, commission salespeople, and retired military people masquerading as trust officers in some financial institutions.

You do not have to be lonely, either. You are part of an enormous peer group. There are over 25 million of you, and your number is growing. So are your options. You will be around for a long time, so do it right and make it exciting. You just might step into the happiest quarter century of your life.

Most of us do not plan for retirement or widowhood. It just happens. Many of my retired clients have discussed with me the emotional and financial consequences of uninformed decisions—how they had failed to understand their options and had not known where or when to seek competent help. We felt there must be an efficient, inexpensive approach to this problem. Planning is a practical start. Plan your retirement well, and it should be an exhilarating experience that will launch you into an exciting new age.

Start now to make checklists for retirement at least a year in advance. Your checklists should include the following (and anything else that will be essential to your own personal dream):

1. A complete and detailed analysis of the current, valid, realistic fair-market value of your assets. These assets might include:
   a. Your home and its contents
   b. Jewelry
   c. Non-income-producing investments such as group ventures in real estate, coin collections, stamp collections

2. A list of every source from which you will receive any income, such as:
   a. Social Security for you and your spouse
   b. Part-time work (if it is in your planning)
   c. Pension and profit-sharing plans from your employment (list all options)
   d. All dividends from investments
   e. All rents from real estate
   f. All income from bank deposits, certificates of deposit, bonds, and the like

g. Consultation in the field in which you have spent your working life (an untapped source of income for many retired executives)

3. A detailed list of your current living expenses. Include:
   a. Approximate current costs of food and medicines and drugs not covered by insurance
   b. Rents
   c. Taxes (real estate, estimated income-tax installment payments)
   d. General maintenance of your home (repairs and utilities)
   e. Automobile maintenance, clothing, and all such related expenses

Once these lists are completed, start to analyze your financial position. One of the most common errors people make is failing to plan to minimize their general overhead and maximize their income once they have retired.

Where can you save money? Consider such questions as these: Is your home now too large for you and your spouse? Could you sell it at a substantial profit and purchase a smaller, easier to maintain garden apartment or other more practical lodging? This might result in small payments or no payments at all, and would certainly minimize your repair and maintenance bills and perhaps provide you with some additional funds for investment.

Is there good reason to buy a new car just because you have retired? Your income is going to be limited now. If you do need a new car, consider the purchase of a compact model.

Look for the most profitable way to amass assets that will produce income once your salary stops. It is essential that you start putting aside some of your salary during the last fifteen or twenty years of work, which will be used for investments to replace your salary once you retire. Unfortunately, many of today's middle-class employed will in retirement be tomorrow's poverty class if they do not plan to replace their income long before they retire. It strikes me as prudent to look for the most profitable way to invest your savings—one that will produce some income and assure a modest hedge against inflation once your salary stops.

Take time now and consider how you will live without your income. Assuming that your needs will diminish in retirement, you will still have to replace somewhere between 50 and 70 percent of your salary, once you retire. This means you will have to have enough assets invested to produce an income that will represent the portion of your missing salary you will need to support yourself once you retire.

There are two distinct financial problems the average retiree must face. The first is gathering sufficient assets for investment in your pre-retirement years; the second is the prudent management of these assets, once you retire. In both instances you should seek your own independent professional adviser. It is essential that the self-employed visit their accountant or tax attorney and consider establishing an independent retirement plan, available under the ERISA law. Under this law the self-employed can set up an Individual Retirement Account (IRA), and invest up to $1,500 off the top of his or her income without paying any income tax, and invest this money into a retirement plan. You can also establish a Keogh Plan, which is a similar idea but allows the self-employed to set aside as much as $7,500 a year free of income tax, during their working years. Keogh Plans must be maintained every year and can be a problem for those with volatile incomes. The Individual Retirement Account, on the other hand, can be used every year, but you are not forced to do it in bad years.

I cannot emphasize too strongly the importance of preretirement planning and the gathering of income-producing assets for retirement. The earlier you start, the better you will be. All persons over age forty-five should be aware that once they retire they must replace the salary they will lose with something else. Social Security and most pension plans will not be enough. In addition to the gathering of investable assets, once you are ready for retirement, you might sell some of your collectibles. For example, a houseful of antiques collected over the years might be sold for a substantial amount of money. If you have an old Tiffany lamp lying around, you could almost retire on that alone. Don't assume that your old things are junk: They may have substantial hidden value. Your new residence may not house all these things, and selling them could produce investment capital. Place the funds thus realized into a secure income-producing investment that will slowly grow, be a hedge against inflation, and augment your retirement income.

If you have any old, inactive savings accounts, check on them at once, especially if you have moved and have not changed your address on those accounts. Many states have laws relating to inactive accounts, and after many years of nonuse your account might become part of some school fund or other public institution if you do not reclaim it in time.

Carefully consider what assets you have that do not produce a fair and reasonable income. Perhaps it would be prudent to dispose of them now. While you are still working you have the income to pay the capital-gains taxes that might accrue from the sale of these assets.

Eliminate all risk equities from your portfolio. You want to maintain and preserve your assets. Once you retire, it is no longer prudent to risk loss while seeking additional growth. Solidify and maximize your income and learn to live within that income. Once you accept this position, freedom from financial worries will make your retirement much more comfortable. There are many conservative, income-producing securities and equities available for the retired.

Once you retire, do not liquidate *all* your assets and put *all* your monies into a nongrowth annuity or savings account. These steps could spell disaster down the road if inflation continues. You must maintain the dollar value of your principal and the purchasing power of your dollar. This is the area where most mistakes are made. Too much cash in savings accounts, thought to be a secure investment, is in fact a loss—a guaranteed loss. Savings accounts lose money through the ravages of inflation.

Since this is the first time in your life that you have completely free choice to do whatever you want, whenever you want, and also the first time you no longer need to save money, *you can and should live on all of your income.* I stress this because many retired people continue to save part of their income out of fear or habit. Your income is limited in retirement. You should see that you get the most income available, then *use it all.* To do otherwise is wasteful: You not only limit your life style, you also increase estate costs and estate taxes at your death.

Many of my retired clients feel that when they were younger and healthier they failed to anticipate medical problems that might come later in their lives. It is the one area where many of them most regret the lost opportunity to save money. It is essential that you have a complete physical examination while you are still employed and covered by group insurance. If you will require any operations in the near future, have them while you are in generally good health and employed, and when you are protected with group medical insurance. Although most medical and health insurance policies do not provide 100 percent coverage, you should still use them to your maximum advantage while they exist. Visit your optometrist, ophthalmologist, and dentist; these are areas where the retired have many problems, and these services cost more if they are ignored. If your medical insurance doesn't cover all the expenses, take the deductions from your income tax for the bills you pay. If you wait until you have no income from which to deduct, you will lose 100 percent of the monies you paid for medical expenses. Be sure your physical condition is good before you retire. Remember also that as we get older our nutritional needs change. You might consult a dietician if you have problems.

You may want to consider moving to a different, perhaps warmer, climate once you retire. When you reach retirement age there will be only one or two of you to consider. Your sons and daughters are usually independent, so you are a free agent. Do not burden yourself with the need to live next to your children. They need their freedom and you deserve yours. With modern communication and transportation systems you can live anywhere in the United States and still keep in touch with your family. But again, plan carefully.

## 2. YOUR LIFE INSURANCE

Once you retire, you will probably ask yourself, "How did I get so broke?" Perhaps you will spend more than your limited income. But have you considered all your unnecessary expenses? For example, life insurance can be a trap for the retired.

Do you remember when you first bought your life insurance? You didn't think you could afford it, but social pressure and the persistent salesperson convinced you that you had a duty to provide for the education of your children if you died too soon. (Insurance companies still run the same type of advertisement.) You also felt that you had to protect your wife with insurance because you had nothing else. So you bought that expensive policy and felt good about yourself. Now, thirty to forty years later, you still have this policy and pay for it out of your retirement income. The life insurance industry spends millions on advertising to promote the idea that to die without life insurance ranks with kicking your mother and stepping on the flag. It does not.

There are many alternatives to life insurance once you retire. To understand this better, it is important for you to remember why you bought life insurance in the first place. At that time it was probably as security for your family in case you died too soon. But certainly by now the need to raise and educate your children is gone. If by the time you've retired you still have nothing else—no assets, no stocks, no real estate, no cash or bonds—keep your insurance and go on to the next chapter. But for those who have saved, invested, and managed to put something aside, the need for insurance at this stage of your life is questionable. (The one exception is if you have nonliquid assets and a taxable estate; then you might need insurance to pay estate taxes.)

There are two common types of life insurance, with many variations. One popular form is *term insurance*. Term insurance policies have no cash surrender value and are never paid up; you must make premium payments every year for the rest of your life. Term insurance is much cheaper than whole life policies when you are young, but the premium becomes more expensive as you age. You can't do much to improve retirement income with term insurance policies except terminate them as soon as possible. Most term insurance is purchased for a temporary period, or is bought for a limited and particular purpose, and should not be retained throughout your life.

However, as a result of the Tax Reform Act of 1976, one of the few methods left for passing assets to heirs relatively free of the now burdensome Federal Estate Tax is to make a gift of a term insurance policy on your life. You can name a husband, wife, or child the owner of an insurance policy on your life. The total value and premiums will be included in your taxable estate if you don't live for three years beyond the date of completing the gift. If you live beyond the three-year period, only the annual premiums for the last three years of your life and their total pro rata share in relation to the entire amount of the policy will be included in your taxable estate.

You can also remove the entire policy from your taxable estate (thus saving your family substantial estate taxes) by making a gift of the policy ownership to your beneficiary. In other words, name your beneficiary as the owner of the policy on the policy itself. Thereafter, do not make the annual premium payments yourself. Rather, make a gift of a cash amount each year to your beneficiary and let the new owner pay for the policy with his or her own money. (The annual gift of the cash to pay the premium on the policy must be less than $3,000 in order to avoid gift taxation problems.) If you wish to make such a gift of term insurance, it is essential that you obtain professional assistance from your own estate-tax lawyer or CPA. Gifts, gift taxation, and estate taxes are far too complicated for the layperson. You should seek expert professional assistance before using this vehicle. For example, if your marriage is shaky it might not make sense to transfer ownership of your life insurance policy.

Many employers have term life insurance policies on their former employees. This type of insurance has no cash surrender value, so if you don't make the annual payments on the premiums, by all means keep this insurance. Most people have named their spouse as first beneficiary and their children as alternate beneficiaries on company policies. It is possible today to increase your advantage with such a policy by making these individuals the *owners* of that policy. The same office that manages the retirement section of your company usually handles the insurance. Write and ask for a change-of-ownership form. Tell them you wish to make your spouse (or, of course, your children if you have no spouse) the *owner* of the policy as well as the beneficiary.

The other type of insurance is called *whole life insurance*. It costs the most and pays the highest commissions. If you are imprudent and plan to keep your policy forever, this is probably the kind to buy. When you buy a whole life insurance policy, a small—indeed, a most modest—stipend is put aside by the insurance company for you out of each premium payment. You own this money. It is called the *cash surrender value*. Most insurance companies do not pay any interest to you for keeping and using your money. This type of insurance is sold with the sales pitch that your money is available for an emergency. Retirement *is* that emergency—and you want to increase your retirement income.

There is often a better and less expensive way to provide money for your spouse without that additional loss through inflation which is inevitable with insurance. You might also be able to receive some benefit from the intelligent use of your insurance monies while you live.

Many people don't realize that if they have a $50,000 thirty- to forty-year-old life insurance policy, they probably have close to a $25,000 cash surrender value in that policy by the time they retire. Have you inquired to find out just how much is in yours? Why not do it now? That money is yours; you own it. If you terminate the policy, you can take that money out now and put it into a conservative income-producing investment. In addition, you will not be paying premiums out of your limited retirement income.

If you are concerned about your health and do not want to terminate the policy, you can still use the cash surrender money. You can borrow this money from the insurance company at an interest rate that is usually less than bank rates and invest it. You do not want to spend your reduced and limited income paying premiums for something you do not really need. Your old policy should have a substantial built-up cash surrender value. If you cannot bring yourself to take this money and terminate the policy, at least use your cash surrender value to buy a paid-up policy and don't waste any more of your income on premiums. However, I consider this a last resort, and a bad use of money.

Make a list of all insurance policies you own today. Analyze them with an estate planner, such as an estate-tax lawyer, to see if you can convert these policies to your advantage. Your insurance agent is *not* necessarily the expert to do this for you, because he or she will lose commissions if you terminate your policies.

Don't forget that you probably purchased the insurance to protect your family in case of your premature death. If your children are grown by the time you retire they might not need your life insurance. You also do not receive any benefit from these policies while you live and neither does your spouse. By the time you die, inflation will have shrunk this policy to a fraction of its original value.

Remember too, that $25,000 cash surrender money taken out of your insurance policy, earning a minimum 6 percent income a year from a conservative investment, could give you an additional $1,500 a year in spendable income. This is nothing to sneeze at! Obviously, it is more if your cash surrender value is more. Some of this extra income might even be tax exempt; your broker can assist you here. In addition to the added income you now receive, you will save the money you otherwise might have spent to make annual or semiannual premium payments. So in reality not only will you increase your spendable income during retirement by $1,500 from the income you can receive from the prudent investment of the money in your old cash surrender policy, you will also have additional income to spend which would otherwise have been used to pay for the insurance premiums. Most important, your former insurance money will not shrink in value through inflation.

Many people don't realize that if you have a whole life insurance policy that will pay approximately $50,000 on your death, by the time you reach retirement age you will have a cash surrender value of approximately $25,000. If you die, and the policy pays the $50,000 face insured amount, *you do not receive the cash surrender value money in addition to the $50,000.* In other words, the $25,000 cash surrender value is lost. It is retained by the insurance company; so, in effect, they do not pay you $50,000—they pay your heirs

$25,000 plus the $25,000 which is yours before you die, to make up the $50,000 total. This is an area that is greatly abused by insurance companies. The day before you die you can take that $25,000 out; the day after you die it is lost to you. It would be so much more prudent to take the money now that is yours. The $25,000 will no doubt grow over the years, be a hedge against inflation, and be worth more than $25,000 by the time you die.

If you need additional insurance, buy cheap term insurance. Many people are retiring at a younger age nowadays, at sixty to sixty-five years. If you are in good health, you can still buy term life insurance. Term life insurance does not have cash surrender value (which, by the way, pays minimum interest); but you no longer need that cash surrender value money to be retained by the insurance company.

Be very careful not to transfer the ownership of your regular, *whole* life insurance that has a built-up cash surrender value without expert tax advice. You might incur gift taxes if you do. I feel most people who transfer the ownership of life insurance policies to their beneficiaries and then live more than three years thereafter will be able to save estate taxation of their life insurance. However, if you are ill and might not live for more than three years after the transfer date, you might increase your estate taxes. Be careful how you make these transfers. Any advice given here should be carefully checked with a competent counselor to make the proper adaptation to your own needs. In addition, if you retire your life insurance without expert advice, you might in the rare instance suffer a small income-tax liability. I don't wish to become too technical at this point; nor do I wish to prevent you from cashing in the insurance. Most people can cash in their insurance policies without any liability. The possibility that a modest income tax might fall due should be analyzed by an expert. In any event, the tax is usually *most* modest. You should not automatically be put off with the thought of a tax if retiring the policy will result in better use of your insurance monies to improve your economic situation in retirement.

Discussions in this book on technical areas such as taxes (gift, estate, inheritance, and income taxes), estate planning, law, and so on, must of course, by their very nature, be presented in a very simplified manner. For your own particular needs you should seek the advice of a *qualified expert*: an estate attorney or a certified public accountant (CPA). This is not an area for self-help, for most laypersons do not have the knowledge to handle these affairs without competent assistance. Your insurance agent might not be the proper expert in this instance. He or she will be happy to assist you—if he or she can convince you to purchase an annuity immediately. Don't do it. Most annuities are absurd. You would be well advised to ignore the advertisements that scream at you, "How would you like a guaranteed income for life?" You might as well keep the insurance for all the advantage you receive from annuities. They are every bit as bad as savings accounts, if not worse. Both depreciate constantly, daily, through inflation.

Decisions about whether to continue or cancel life

insurance must not be taken lightly. You should consider all human and economic factors. For example, what is the tolerance of your family if you cancel your life insurance coverage? It would be regrettable to cause unnecessary family problems in retirement. You should provide adequately for your family. There are, of course, other ways than insurance, such as joint assets, living trusts, pension plans, and so on, which will all be discussed further on. You must also provide an adequate cash flow for your retirement needs and for the needs of your family at your death. If your estate will be taxable, your executor might need insurance monies for liquidity at your death.

Should you decide to make better use of your insurance monies than you can by retaining the insurance policies, there are many choices. If you do not need the insurance monies for investment, but don't wish to continue premium payments with your limited retirement income, you can, as an alternative to giving the policy away by gift, reduce that existing policy to a paid-up policy. Many consider this an imprudent use of monies, particularly if high inflation continues. Inflation decreases the value of insurance monies at an alarming rate. On the other hand, if life insurance is the only method by which you can adequately protect your family, there are still other choices. You should receive help from an independent, qualified expert before making any decisions. If you receive your information from those who work on commissions, some options that do not provide maximum commissions might be unintentionally overlooked.

If you have not already done so, it is most important

to examine and review all your insurance policies immediately. No matter what kind of insurance you have, be sure to give your beneficiaries all the insurance in one lump-sum payment at your death. (This does not apply to death benefits from employment, which are discussed elsewhere.) It is imprudent of you and humiliating to your beneficiaries not to. When you limit your spouse to monthly payments, he or she loses money, while the insurance companies earn huge amounts of income from your money, which they often hold without paying any interest or, at best, pay the most minimal interest. The monthly payments they make to your beneficiary are ridiculously small, and their buying power decreases daily through inflation. Your spouse and children also lose any possible chance of growth or investment with this money. All growth investment and increased values are retained by the insurance company.

Make sure your policies read "Option One," which is usually the option referring to lump-sum payment. Look for the words, "One Lump-Sum Payment," and circle that choice. (If you are not sure, address this specific question to your insurance agent.) Your spouse can then purchase a conservative investment with this money. More often than not, the income earned by the conservative stock will exceed the monthly payments made by most insurance companies. In any event, the purchasing power of your dollar will not decrease daily. I cannot emphasize too strongly the absurdity of allowing insurance companies to hold your money and use it without paying a fair interest.

*Don't Die Broke!*

This section on alternate uses of insurance applies only to the retired and soon to be retired. If you are a younger person, chances are that nothing can replace your insurance or do the job that insurance will do to provide monies for your family. Also, this section only applies to the retired who have other assets in addition to insurance.

# 3. YOUR EXPERT ADVISER

You would be well advised to seek an attorney in your community whose practice is substantially limited to tax-estate planning. There are lawyers in every community who specialize in or limit their practice to this field. You can ask an attorney if he is a member of the Estate Planning Council in his community. If he is not, you can assume that he is not a full-time estate planner.

There are reference books that identify lawyers who practice in different areas of law, and a book called *The American Probate Directory* lists estate-planning or probate lawyers. You might also visit the county courthouse at your county seat and ask the Clerk of Court to let you examine the ledgers where probates are filed. They are usually maintained on an annual basis. Read through the list for the past year and make note of the lawyers' names. You will find certain names repeated; these are the lawyers who work constantly in estate planning and probate and do not expect to retire on the proceeds of probating one estate. You can assume that they treat each estate with the respect it deserves. Remember that the fee you will pay for expert advice is no more than for inexpert advice and will usually save large amounts of money and make your retirement substantially more comfortable.

A competent and honest attorney does not earn commissions. He is not interested in selling you expensive 8 percent commissioned mutual funds (which the retired should not buy anyway), and he will not sell you a trust if the yearly cost of the trust will be too expensive for the services you receive. He should not be interested in anything except serving you at a reasonable hourly fee. Your interest is his interest, and there should be no hidden profits for him.

You will need a proper estate plan and a will. Wills that are more than five years old are often expensive to use and usually do not reflect your most recent wishes. If a living trust is advisable, your attorney will analyze that picture with you. See Part Five on trusts in this book, which discusses this subject in depth and will help you understand your lawyer's advice.

Once you find your expert, ask him or her to analyze your insurance with you to see if it is worthwhile to terminate the coverage. This attorney can also help you make the proper choice on your pension or profit-sharing plan. If you have listed your assets, analyzed your position, and understood the concepts in this book, you will be able to discuss your options intelligently at that time.

One regrettable problem in some retirement communities is that most retirees who move to these places have no local sources of reference when they seek an attorney. They are invited into the trust department of a local bank where a trust officer is alleged to "interview" them. He then "recommends" a local attorney.

Unfortunately, trust officers in some banks in some retirement communities, recommend the same three or four lawyers. Coincidentally, these three or four lawyers have until quite recently been trust officers in these same banks. They have left their bank positions to practice law and have established quite successful practices with remarkable speed. There would appear to be a painful private relationship between some bank trust officers in some retirement communities and some former bank employees or ex-trust officers. The present trust officers "recommend" their former associates whose suggestions parallel those of the banks. The bank will then reward the former trust officer when your estate is administered by hiring him or her and paying legal fees.

There are a number of competent attorneys in all communities. You must protect yourself by asking why some trust departments seem to limit their recommendations to their former colleagues. You can demand that they recommend *all* the competent lawyers in your community, even those who were not former trust officers with the bank.

It is difficult and dangerous to define an expert. I feel that anyone with a professional degree or training can become an expert in a particular field in time. But be aware that a title such as "lawyer" or "CPA" or "accountant" or "doctor" simply means that someone is academically qualified (which is, indeed, most important); it does not mean that that person always has the experience or integrity to be called "expert."

It strikes me as basic that before anyone blindly follows advice, one must first ask two questions: First,

"What is the specific nature of this person's profession-al expertise?" After all, lawyers don't necessarily know much about taxes, a CPA doesn't usually know the law, and bank tellers know neither. Second, "What is this person's experience?" A CPA and/or lawyer with ten years of experience as an estate planner/tax specialist and knowledge of pension and profit-sharing plans, certainly might merit my full attention if I wanted a will, a trust, or advice in preretirement planning for legal and tax information. It is regrettable that so few of us pick the right person for the right job. The individual over fifty cannot afford to make such mis-takes.

# 4. THE PENSION PLAN

Company pension plans and profit-sharing plans are very complicated. Choosing a payment option from such a tax-qualified retirement plan requires serious study. In general, such plans are established wherein tax-free funds are set aside by your employer on your behalf while you are working. These funds grow and earn income, all of which is income-tax free while you work. Once you retire and choose a payment option, you will pay an income tax on the monies from these funds when you receive them. How you are taxed and how much income tax you will pay is determined by a number of factors: the number of years you were employed prior to retirement; the type of payments you receive; the kind of contribution you made to the plan out of your own income.

For example, in some instances you can choose to have all or a varying percentage of the monies you receive taxed as income or in part as capital gains. If you choose to have it all taxed as straight income and if you meet other qualifications, you can have what is known as a "ten year carry forward" so that the income you receive after retirement from these plans will be taxed on a ten-year basis at your then low retirement income level. Whether this form of taxation is better for you, or if a partial income tax and partial capital-gains tax is preferable, can only be determined by your own accountant. Some plans require that you choose an option as early as a year before you retire. It strikes me as eminently sensible to look at the variety of options under your plan and have an independent professional person analyze their meaning, tax qualifications, and options with you, far in advance of the time you have to make a choice.

A few companies offer excellent and very inexpensive options with their retirement plans. Notable are plans of the New York City school system, du Pont, and the federal government. These seem to have fair, reasonable, and indeed most inexpensive options in the form of continued annuity-type payments for a surviving spouse and a standard-of-living clause that will increase the benefits if, and as, the cost of living increases in the future. Unfortunately, too few companies offer such fair plans.

In my opinion the second most abused area for the retired, after insurance, concerns advice about choosing among the options available under company retirement plans. The executive in charge of these plans is, first, a company person, whose interest lies at least as much in protecting the company as in protecting you. You must recognize that some people who offer advice might have ulterior motives, and their motivation must be analyzed before you seek or follow their advice.

Most corporate attorneys are employees of the corporation and are very competent. Nevertheless, their

specialty is corporation law; generally, their knowledge of estate planning and taxes and of retirement
problems is zero! They may well know less about these
problems than you do. Their dispensing advice is a
perfect example of the blind leading the blind.

In your preretirement years you should analyze all
the options available in your particular retirement
plan. Most corporations have retirement plans, and
the majority of such plans usually offer a variety of
payment choices. Three of the most common choices
in most plans are the following:

1. Lump sum payment, where you take everything
all at once in the form of one payment

2. Payment of a certain percentage of the funds to
which you are entitled for a guaranteed number of
years—for example, a ten-year guaranteed payment

3. An annuity-type payment; for example, two typical annuity choices found in many plans are:

a. 100 percent of your retirement benefits in the
form of a monthly income to you for your lifetime,
with no continuation for your family once you die

b. Less than 100 percent, possibly 75 percent,
taken on a monthly payment, and an agreed upon
percentage of your benefits (less than what you have
been receiving) to be paid to your surviving spouse in
monthly payments for the rest of his or her lifetime;
this is called a joint and survivor annuity payment.

Unfortunately, many employees tend to pick an option that results in a smaller number of payments than
they could otherwise receive. Choosing complicated
and technical retirement plan options without first

obtaining assistance in analyzing your personal needs and without independent analysis of each option, strikes me as reckless. Also, this is not the time to do what others think would be right. It is the time to analyze carefully and realistically what your income and family needs will be during your retirement, and then to opt for the payment best suited to these needs.

Each of these pension plan options has a specific tax meaning. If you don't understand the tax meanings, you should have these options and methods of payment analyzed by your own tax attorney or CPA long before you must exercise a choice, so that you can choose the one that will best fit your family needs. The money you will pay your own professional adviser to help you make these choices can result in thousands of dollars of additional payments to you and your surviving spouse once you retire or die.

Most corporations have millions of (tax free) dollars in unused assets in the form of pension and profit-sharing plans. These plans enjoy their greatest increase when individuals give up half their justly earned monies. Perhaps someday some congressional committee will rectify this outrage, but in the interim you must protect yourself.

Generally, unless you are five years or more older than your spouse, you should not automatically take the smallest income in an attempt to protect him or her after your death. There are many other factors to consider before you make a choice, among them:

1. Does your spouse have separate assets?
2. Does your spouse have a pension or profit-sharing plan of his or her own?

3. Will your spouse inherit anything from someone else?

4. If your spouse is sick and your health is good, his or her life expectancy might be substantially less than yours, and it would probably not be wise to give up half your income to protect him or her under these circumstances.

5. If you are both healthy and you retire young enough still to be insurable, you might consider an additional alternative—but only as a last choice. Find a life insurance agent and ask him how much term life insurance you can buy with an amount of money *equal to* what you would let the company keep if you took less than 100 percent of your retirement income.

Point 5 is not inconsistent with my statements in Chapter 2, where you were advised to consider terminating your insurance. This is an entirely different situation. You might be in a better economic position if you take 100 percent of your retirement benefits and use some of that money to purchase term insurance on your life to protect your spouse if you die first and want additional assets for him or her. At your death, the new term insurance policy could mean a cash sum for your spouse, who could then use the insurance money to purchase an additional income-producing utility stock or bond. This might well produce more income for him or her than the continued payments from the 50 percent of your retirement income, the purchasing power of which would have depreciated annually through inflation. All fixed incomes from pension plans constantly depreciate; their purchasing power is less every single year. Very few pension plans have a cost-of-living increase factor built into them, so very few of them will pay more as the cost of living increases. If your spouse is to maintain his or her standard of living, it is essential that you find a way to beat the inflation factor.

For example, if that portion of your retirement funds that you would have left with your company can purchase a term life insurance policy in the amount of $30,000 or more, you can probably make substantial gains for your family. Suppose you take 100 percent of your retirement income, but live only on the amount you would have received if you had taken a lesser plan and buy term life insurance with the amount of money you otherwise would have let your company keep. You will not *use* all of your 100 percent retirement income, and that portion of the income equal to that which you would have let the company keep will make payments on a new term insurance policy on your life. This is a method whereby you can greatly increase your estate without losing any of your retirement funds. If you take 100 percent benefits under your retirement plan and purchase a term policy, your heirs will receive that money when you die. By this approach, you hedge and cover your flanks.

In other words, if you choose to take 50 percent of the income to which you are entitled on retirement and your spouse dies first, you lose money. You continue living on less income than you could otherwise receive and your family will receive nothing when you die. On the other hand, if you opt for 100 percent of your retirement income (even though it will end at your death) and then purchase a term life insurance policy with 50 percent of that income, you will be no worse off for funds than you would be taking the lesser plan, and this way you have the insurance, your spouse is protected, and your estate increases.

If your spouse should die before you, you have still another choice. Since you will receive 100 percent of your retirement income, you can raise your standard of living: Cancel the term insurance policy and live on all your income. By choosing 100 percent of your retirement income, you will continue to receive that amount until you die. In this manner, you will receive the maximum income-producing factor throughout your retirement.

It might well be, however, that you need a retirement plan that will give you less income than 100 percent of your benefits but will permit you to protect your spouse. If you are uninsurable or if your spouse is ill or cannot manage money, the only practical way might be to take less than 100 percent from your retirement plan and have some form of payment continue to your spouse after your death. This is an expensive road to take, but it could possibly be your only choice. Only an impartial adviser can analyze this for you. This is just one additional but important consideration before you make a retirement choice. Don't forget that the name of the game is to get the maximum amount of income once you retire. Why should you automatically take a minimum amount if you can better your situation with valid planning before you retire?

Company benefits for employees are complex and involve both income-tax and estate-tax considerations.

Today, "carry-over pensions" to a surviving spouse can be taxed as income to the spouse. Lump-sum death payments to your heirs will also now be taxed to your estate unless you have a nontaxable estate. If your estate will be taxed at your death, you can remove the death benefits paid by your company from taxation if you choose an option that will have the money paid in at least three annual installments to your spouse rather than a lump sum. While it would appear imprudent to give your spouse monthly payments from your pension or insurance and thus lose all growth potential from the use of the monies, it might nevertheless make sense to choose an option for company death benefits that will give your spouse three annual payments and thereby remove the total amount from your taxable estate. In my opinion (assuming reasonable health by both husband and wife), in most situations in which both husband and wife are employed and each will receive an individual pension, each should take 100 percent of their individual benefits.

Assume that husband can take 100 percent or $250 a month; or if he takes $125 a month, wife will continue to receive that amount if he dies. Assume wife has similar rights for $200 a month, or $100 and $100 carry-over for husband if she dies. If both take the maximum, they receive a total of $450 a month or $5,400 a year, exclusive of all other rights from Social Security and the like. (Statistics show that the average retired couple lives more than ten years in retirement. However, for simplicity, let us use ten-year averages.) In ten years, they will take out of the company plans a total of $54,000. If they each took half to protect the spouse, they would have only received a total of $27,000 in ten years. Their ten year loss of income is $27,000—$2,700 per year or $225 a month.

Assume husband dies after only ten years. Wife will take her own $100 a month and another $125 from husband's carry-over for a monthly total of $225. However, she could have taken $200 a month from her own plan, so in reality she only makes an extra $25 a month from the husband's plan. She will have to live as a widow for ninety years to make up the lost $27,000. Had they each taken the maximum amount from their individual plans, with no carry-over for the spouse, and had only lived on one-half the amount they received, they could have invested the other one-half or $27,000. Put into a simple savings account, the $27,000 would be worth a minimum of $38,000, so at the husband's death, the wife could have her own $200 a month income, plus the income from the $38,000 in a time certificate of deposit (which in my opinion is not a safe hedge against inflation). Nevertheless, interest at a mere 6 percent will produce another $180 income per month for a total of $380 per month for the widow. And she still owns the $38,000 to leave as an estate for the children. The misuse of pension plan options is an outrage. And the husband could never make up his loss either, if the wife were to die first.

## 5. THE RETIREMENT HOME

There are approximately 50,000 or more retired residents in the neighboring retirement communities of Sun City and Youngtown, Arizona, where I practice law. There were about 700 residents when I opened my office; it is anticipated that 70,000 residents will probably live here by 1980. Most of them will come from other states and from foreign countries. Most people live and work with the idea that upon retirement they will move to a worry-free Shangri-la in the sunshine. There is, of course, no such place. You take your problems wherever you go—and new ones may develop.

Retirement abruptly changes one's social status. Many officers in the Armed Services, corporation executives, or active professionals earn substantial incomes while they work and are also in positions of authority. Once they retire, they are suddenly, and probably for the first time in many years, without authority, social status, or direction. This can be shattering to the ego. Thus, in addition to the humiliation of money problems, real or imagined, there is a need to prepare for an assault on your self-image. Proper planning can minimize emotional shock and allow you to adjust gradually, gracefully, and enjoyably to your new situation.

In the community where you live and work you are well known and liked by your friends. They respect you and after your retirement will still consider you the friend, the chief, the director, the adviser. You will continue to receive much of the respect you had in the past and need so desperately once you retire. But if you move immediately to a new environment where you are unknown, the impact of a changed economic position in conjunction with a new social position may be an overwhelming burden. It is the rare person indeed who can accept both upheavals at once. If you move immediately to your spot in the sunshine and are completely unknown there, you may find it difficult to survive the emotional trauma. So don't sever your ties too abruptly or completely. You might plan to spend the first few months of your retirement among your family and friends. Enjoy your new freedom: do the things you always wanted to do; find new interests; develop a hobby.

When your first retirement winter approaches, visit your dream spot in the sunshine. Do not buy at once, but rent or lease a place for the season. If you lease, you know that you have not completely cut your ties and that you can always go home again. You will not feel insulated and isolated. Slowly and at your own pace you can see if you are ready for a change of environment. After living in a new environment for six months to a year, you will know if you like it well enough to stay. If you do, purchase your new home and move—but very slowly. A substantial number of new residents in retirement communities move back to their former homes. Those who no longer have cash or who will lose too much money on the resale of their "retirement home" are often stuck—and miserable. The suicide rate, alcoholic rate, and shoplifting rate are all increasing in every retirement community. It is a sad, shocking commentary on haste. If you move slowly and graciously, you can adapt.

Retirement communities offer many advantages. However, if you drive through the sunshine states you will also see isolated, badly maintained buildings by the side of the road, in the middle of nowhere. These are retirement homes in communities that were never finished. The developer was not financially secure and went bankrupt. The buyers are stuck, because they cannot resell these homes. To avoid this fate, check very carefully into the financial background of any corporation that develops a retirement community in which you are interested. You can do this by inquiring at the Corporation Commission office in most states. Don't waste your savings! Be sure you purchase in a well-developed community. You will not lose your money or your investment if you consider only already established communities.

If you rent a place for the season in a retirement community, you might consider leasing your present home. It certainly doesn't pay to leave it empty, and you would not want to sell it until you were sure you would not want to return. There might be an economic advantage in retaining your original home if you can buy a new one in a retirement community without the monies you would receive from the sale of your old one. You can then turn your old home into an investment. You can lease the house, receive a monthly income, and depreciate the house, since it is now an investment. The depreciation schedule will be such that most of the rent you receive in the form of income will be nontaxable to you for many years. You might have your financial adviser or accountant go over these facts and figures with you. This opportunity to receive tax-free income to help you in your retirement is often ignored.

If you plan to rent your old home, be sure to check with your insurance company so that your home-owner's policy will cover you for rentals. Some policies do not; other policies specifically exclude coverage for renters. On the other hand, if you plan to leave your present home empty while you visit retirement communities for about six months, check to see that your present homeowner's insurance policy will still cover you. Some deny coverage if a residence is left empty.

Many charities are getting into the retirement business by running retirement nursing homes and apartments. You purchase the right to live in such an apartment. They are quite expensive—between $20,000 and $40,000. You don't receive ownership or title to the apartment for this money. All you receive is an alleged lifetime use of the apartment. In addition to this fee, you will pay a monthly maintenance fee for food and the right to use all the facilities. Among the advertised facilities are "complete medical care for the rest of your life."

Some of my clients live in such communities, and

after a number of years in residence they find that their complaints are increasing. It would appear that few of these centers can truly afford to provide the complete medical services they advertise. There are few full-time physicians and rarely any specialists. If you need medical treatment that requires a specialist, you must provide and pay for this yourself, unless you are covered through insurance. The medical facilities are often crowded and sometimes uncomfortable. Moreover, some such organizations appear to attempt to declare their residents incompetent at the first possible opportunity. Another complaint has been that some communities move elderly, ill, widowed persons into the infirmary, telling them they are too sick to live alone. They must therefore live the rest of their days in the infirmary. This allows the charity to resell the apartment to another individual immediately, even though the previous apartment dweller is still alive. If you think a retirement center is what you want, you would be wise to talk with a number of residents at centers you are considering and be sure that none of the above-mentioned abuses are prevalent there.

If you move to a retirement community or just a different part of town, choose a place that is not isolated, far out of town. Be sure you are at a convenient spot close to public transportation and other facilities. As you become older and lose your ability to drive, this will become a matter of greatest importance.

# 6. THE SINGLE RETIRED PERSON

Widows, widowers, and unmarried and divorced retired persons share a common problem: Many retirement communities are especially designed for couples. The single person in such a place is often lonely. In addition, some people, as they become older, continue to cast around for new and exciting associations, and in old age some spouses become more jealous, not less. The single retired individual is thus often subjected to automatic suspicion.

Choose a retirement community that provides housing for single retired people as well as for couples, if you plan to move. New retirement communities provide condominium apartments for single individuals, where you will find companionship.

The information provided throughout this book applies to the single retired person, the widow, and the widower, as well as to couples, unless you are otherwise informed in the text. Generally the decisions, the mistakes, the choices, the problems of the widow, the widower, and the single retired person are substantially the same as those of a married couple. A married couple must, of course, plan their retirement together, whereas the single person will do it alone. This is probably the only basic difference between the two cases.

# SUMMARY
# OF
# PART ONE

Plan for retirement carefully. Start at least one year before your retirement begins. Make checklists for retirement. Include the following complete and detailed analysis of your assets (all of which must have a current, valid fair-market value):

1. Your home and its contents
2. Jewelry and uniquely expensive items
3. Non-income-producing investments such as group ventures in real estate
4. Coin and stamp collections
5. Anything else of marketable value

An additional list should detail your income potential, such as:

1. Social Security for you and/or your spouse
2. Part-time work
3. Pension and profit-sharing plans (list all options)
4. All dividends from investments
5. Rents from real estate
6. Income from bank deposits, certificates of deposit, bonds, and the like

7. Consultation in your field
8. Any other source of income that you can anticipate

A final list should include your current living expenses, such as:

1. Approximate budget for food
2. Approximate cost of medicines and drugs not covered by insurance.
3. Rent
4. Taxes (real estate, estimated income, and the like)
5. General maintenance of your home (include repairs and utilities)
6. Other expenses such as automobile maintenance, clothing, and such related items

When your lists are complete, analyze your financial position. This is when you should look to see where you can save money. Try to eliminate all risk equities from your portfolio; the goal is to maintain and preserve your assets.

It is essential that you do not liquidate assets and then put your monies into a nongrowth annuity or a savings account. Such actions could mean economic disaster if inflation continues. You must maintain the dollar value of your principal and the purchasing power of your dollar.

Once your income stops you must receive support from a different source. It is therefore necessary that you save something from your income during the last fifteen or twenty years of your working life, which can be set aside for investments that will produce an income to replace the salary you will lose when you retire. It is highly unlikely that Social Security or modest pension payments will be enough. Most middle class individuals will need to supplement their income from another source in order to maintain a reasonable standard of living during retirement. The self-employed should visit their tax attorney or CPA to see about establishing an independent retirement account or a Keogh Plan. Those who are employed and covered by company group retirement plans will still find it prudent to set aside a modest portion of their income every year for investment so that they can augment the income they will receive from their company pension plans. I do not know of any pension plan that pays you more than 50 percent of your income once you retire. It is therefore absolutely necessary that you prepare a supplemental source of income for yourself once you retire. Clearly, this means you must take something from your income while you work and make conservative, prudent investments. If you do not, you might find yourself among tomorrow's poverty class once you retire.

Once you retire, I believe you should then plan to live on all your income. There is no reason for retired people to limit their enjoyment of life in an attempt to leave estates for their children.

Leave your employment in your best possible physical condition. Complete all physical examinations and any operations you can anticipate while you are employed and covered by group insurance.

Consider whether you really need your life insurance. Are you deriving any benefits from it? Many retired individuals have substantial cash surrender value in their old insurance policies which is lost to them while they live and to their heirs after their death. Consider cashing the policies in and investing the cash surrender value in a conservative income-producing growth investment. This will provide additional income to you and preserve the dollar value of your assets. Insurance policies depreciate daily, shrinking as a result of inflation; therefore, insurance monies have less purchasing power for your heirs when you die. These policies should not be held longer than absolutely necessary. Once you retire, insurance gives you little advantage, unless you need it to pay estate taxes. Often, the reason why you purchased the insurance originally is no longer valid.

Many people pay too much for annual insurance premiums. If your insurance policy has a cash surrender value, this money belongs to you. A $30,000 life insurance policy that is thirty years old could have a $15,000 cash surrender value. Therefore with your premiums you are purchasing only an additional $15,000 worth of insurance, although the amount of your premiums is based on the full $30,000 policy. When you die, the insurance company pays your heirs the $15,000 that is already yours and only $15,000 of their own money. This is an area of great abuse by insurance companies. If you have not already done so, it might be more prudent for you to take your cash surrender money now. If you need additional insurance (and I cannot imagine why you should), purchase inexpensive term insurance to cover the difference between your cash surrender value money and the additional amount you desire.

If your employer has term insurance policies on

your life as a result of your former employment, and you do not have to pay the premiums, keep this insurance.

Find an expert and independent adviser. (This means going outside the company, because most employers do not provide an independent expert to analyze these plans to *your* best advantage.) He will help you plan your retirement intelligently. Any tax-trained, estate-planning attorney is qualified to analyze your assets, do estate planning such as wills and trusts, and analyze the various options available to you in your retirement and pension plans.

Most company retirement pension and profit-sharing plans provide a variety of choices. Each has different tax considerations and represents a substantial amount of monies, well into the thousands of dollars. It makes sense to have your own independent expert analyze the meaning of all these options for you before you make your choice. And you certainly will need outside professional help to determine if your total estate is taxable and whether you must try to remove company death benefits from your taxable estate.

It is often emotionally traumatic to move immediately to a new environment as soon as you retire. Do not sever your ties completely or too abruptly. Visit your dream spot in the sunshine, if you wish. Rent or lease a place there for the season, rather than buying immediately. If you lease, you can always go back home without a serious financial loss; you will not be permanently insulated and isolated. This way you can see if you are ready for the change of environment slowly and without risk. If you like your new retirement home after living there six months to a year on a lease basis, it is probably safe to purchase.

Retirement communities can offer advantages. However, some are on the verge of bankruptcy. Don't waste your savings. Check into the financial background of any corporation that develops a retirement community in which you are interested. Be sure it is solvent, that it has unmortgaged assets. And make sure you purchase in a well-developed area; it is never advisable to be the first to buy into a new retirement community. If the developer does not complete his development, the home you purchased in the undeveloped, uncompleted community will be almost worthless. Above all, *never buy a retirement home without visiting the community in advance.*

If you feel that you might, at one point, have to move into a nursing home, it might make sense to visit all such homes in your community while you are well and competent and can get about. There are a variety of homes. Some are private, others are government-sponsored, and still others are associated with charities and religious organizations. Some require that you pay a substantial entrance fee which is never returned; others require that you buy a lease (which can run into many thousands of dollars) and also pay a monthly rental. Some offer "medical or infirmary facilities" and others have no sheltered care facilities whatsoever. While visiting these homes, you might talk to the present residents and see what complaints they have that will better enable you to make a decision as to the type of home you will want to live in when it is your turn. Ask if you can have a luncheon or supper at these homes. Be sure to check out the food, the health and exercise facilities, and most importantly, the sheltered care facilities. If you must move into a nursing home, it strikes me as sensible to choose one that will have a sheltered care facility that you can move into if the need arises, rather than face the trauma of moving once again to a strange place when you are too ill or weak to make intelligent choices.

Decisions and problems for the widow, the widower, and the unmarried or divorced person are substantially the same as those for a married couple. The information in this book will therefore apply to single individuals as well as to married couples.

**PART TWO:**

# After You Retire

# 7.  EDUCATE
## YOUR
## SPOUSE

In most families either the husband or the wife handles the business affairs; either the wife maintains
records, writes the family checks, and pays the bills, or
the husband does everything. In either case, one
spouse is often completely ignorant of the family's
economic facts. It is the rare family indeed where
husband and wife maintain the records together.

When one individual handles the family assets, the
other spouse is in a completely exposed position.
Therefore, as you approach retirement, you must
educate your spouse. The spouse who handles the
business affairs of the family must take pains to instruct the other how to write checks and keep records.
Prepare a written inventory of what both of you own.
Explain where everything is located, especially jewelry
or anything you have in your own name.

At retirement, both spouses should begin to handle
all family business affairs together. Insist that your
spouse participate; write the checks together; analyze
your problems and needs together; make investment
choices together. It certainly pays to introduce your
spouse to your business adviser, broker, and other

professionals who handle your affairs. Educating your spouse is the most important thing you can do for him or her when you retire. Each partner in a marriage has a duty to tell the other spouse everything about family affairs and a corresponding right to know where all family assets are located.

It is often necessary to show a wife how to maintain herself so that she will not be abused in widowhood. Many men feel that their wives are not capable of handling business affairs. This is absurd! If she is not capable while you live, she will be less capable after you die. Start to instruct her immediately if you haven't already. You abuse your entire family by indulging laziness while you live. Nothing is more pitiful than a worried widow with no knowledge of how to cope with finances (especially if she doesn't know what she owns), in a state of shock after her husband's death. There is no greater cruelty than keeping your wife or husband uninformed.

Many men and women tell their children or a friend where things are, and neglect to tell a spouse. This is regrettable and silly, because the children usually forget, and in any event are the wrong ones to tell. Prepare a written list, with a copy for your personal records, place one copy in your safety deposit box, or give your lawyer a copy to keep in your file in his office.

List the following in detail for each other:

1. All separate and joint assets. Explain what these are in detail, and where they are located.

2. All your securities, such as stocks or bonds. Tell your spouse where the certificates are located. If either of you has a street account with a broker, make sure

your spouse knows the broker, the address of the office handling the account, the account number, and the securities held in the account.

3. All your insurance. Introduce your spouse to the insurance agent. If you haven't done so already, it might be advisable to write your insurance company and ask them to send you a proof-of-death claim now, so that you can keep it attached to your policy; then your survivor will merely have to fill it out at your death. Most insurance companies don't pay interest from the time of death, so the policy should be the first thing any beneficiary turns in.

Also, analyze your wills both with your attorney and with each other. Make sure you both understand everything specified in the wills. Your spouse is the one who will have to live under the terms and conditions of your will and deserves a voice in what you do.

If you live in a state that locks safe-deposit boxes at the death of the owner (and the majority of states do this), take all your insurance papers and your will and put them into a safe-deposit box owned by your spouse, or have your attorney or other adviser hold them for you. In any event, make sure your wife or husband knows where they are and that each of you can get to the other's assets quickly.

It would also appear essential that the spouse who manages the household affairs, shopping, cooking, cleaning, and the like, teach the other spouse some of these talents. Wives do occasionally predecease husbands. When that happens, most men are in a state of panic, and simply do not know how to maintain themselves. They often do not have the basic tools and resources for survival as a single. It strikes me as important that women teach some of their talents to their husbands, so that the men need not be forced into an immediate remarriage.

# 8. YOUR FINANCIAL REEDUCATION

## Don't Speculate with Your Assets

Now that you are retired, money problems will probably be your main concern. Your assets will be in good order if you have taken the time to plan your retirement carefully, but you can no longer afford the luxury of losing money through high-risk investments, because you cannot replace your losses. You must try to protect your standard of living, and this can best be done without reckless speculation in the marketplace.

There is no reason to play the market at this stage in your life. I do not mean that you should sell your good investments. I simply mean that you should stop speculating and stop active trading. If your assets are good stocks—conservative growth stocks or conservative bonds—these are exactly what you need to hedge against inflation and preserve the buying power of your retirement monies. There is, however, no need for active trading once your affairs are in good order. Before you retired, you should have converted all your assets into conservative, high-income-producing stocks or, perhaps, certain bonds. Generally, conservative and preferred stocks do not fluctuate violently as most common stocks do. They provide a fair and reasonable income in the way of dividends, and they occasionally split. Most important, they usually hedge against inflation over any given five-year period. Today the market is substantially different than it was a short time ago. Many economists believe that our economy is in line for a number of volatile market changes with periods of substantial inflation. Investments made during such times should include assets specifically designed to minimize the effects of inflation. For example, most knowledgeable financial institutions reduce their long-term bonds and purchase short-term Treasury obligations if they anticipate inflation.

It is unusual for the average person to have knowledge of changing market conditions or what constitutes a secure investment at any given time. Speculation in the marketplace without expert advice is always dangerous. Regrettably, many brokers are not experts, and commission salespeople are often influenced by a variety of considerations.

Investment counselors often advise people to protect themselves by dividing assets into a variety of secured investments, including short-term Treasury obligations, some bonds, a modest savings account, and the like. The average retired person should be concerned with preservation of assets rather than increasing or building an estate. The preservation of assets in these changing times is most difficult without proper advice. It is often a mistake to liquidate your assets and lay them aside into a nongrowth investment.

Even when the market slumps, most dividends continue. Your income is usually not affected.

Many of your stocks may have increased in value since you purchased them. Some of these stocks are probably not the secure, income-producing, conservative kinds that you should hold once you are retired. Many of my clients express a desire to change these assets but are afraid of having to pay capital-gains taxes. This is a mistake. Most growth stocks pay minimum dividends. It is ridiculous to sit on assets that do not produce a good income just to avoid paying capital-gains taxes. A capital-gains tax means that you have made a profit; you should not be unhappy about that. You should start to sell nonconservative old stocks, a little at a time before retirement, and pay a modest capital-gains tax. You can then purchase a high-income-producing investment that will help you maintain your standard of living.

The Tax Reform Act of 1976 did substantial harm to the historical concept of capital gains. In my opinion the destruction by Congress of the capital-gains concept will probably minimize the availability of investment capital in future generations. There is very little profit left in the investment business. Some congressmen now realize the disaster they inflicted on the investing public with new abusive capital-gains taxes, and it is most surely going to necessitate changes once again in the capital-gains tax law.

Before January 1, 1977, the capital-gains tax was basically quite simple. You would pay a capital-gains tax on profit. This tax was substantially less than regular income tax. For example, if you paid $100 for a security, and sold it for $500, there was a $400 profit, which was subject to a capital-gains tax.

This is no longer the case. As of the date this book is written, the first problem relating to capital-gains taxes is that very few people seem to know what the law says, is, or does. It is so terribly difficult to compute capital-gains taxes today, particularly if you are dealing with real estate, that serious problems are likely to occur, relating to the buying and selling of property.

The tax basis, also called cost basis, (generally meaning the amount paid for property when first purchased and the monies spent for various allowable improvements), will now be computed differently in estates when you are dealing with securities and when you are dealing with real estate. For real estate you must compute your tax basis based upon how long you owned the property before December 31, 1976, and how long you owned the property beyond January 1, 1977. You then perform some intricate, confusing mathematics, worked out by a government formula, and come up with a tax basis that really doesn't resemble at all what you might have paid for the property. For securities, such as stocks and bonds, you are entitled to take for your cost basis the value of the asset on the day you purchased it, or its value on December 31, 1976, whichever is higher. You cannot, however, take the later date for loss on your income tax. Those who inherited assets under the previous law before January 1, 1977, took the value of the property on the date of the death or six months after it for a new tax basis, which often wiped out the deceased person's capital-gains taxes. Today, under the new law, your heirs will take your old tax basis with only a small appreciation.

This new capital-gains section of the Tax Reform Act will probably be changed as soon as the majority of congressmen read it and understand it, but for now it makes sense to seek out a competent CPA to assist you in preparing your income tax if you sold anything during the previous year at a profit or loss. In any event, it certainly doesn't make sense today for you to hold on to your growth securities which do not pay a fair and reasonable income as you approach retirement, just to save a capital-gains tax.

Buy your investments and take title (ownership) in your name alone, unless a tax-trained estate planner tells you it is safe to buy them in the name of yourself and your spouse. Joint assets can have many pitfalls, which are explained in Part Six.

When purchasing mutual funds or stocks, never take title in the name of your offspring as joint owner with you. It is equally imprudent to purchase securities and equities in your name as trustee for someone in your family. The same is true for savings accounts. Keep your assets in your name or in the names of yourself and your spouse and you won't lose them. I don't mean to imply that all children will take their parents' assets. However, the creditors of all children will not hesitate to take parents' assets if the children's names are on the title as joint owners.

There are investment advisers who work mainly to churn your investments for commissions. To justify this manipulation of your assets, some brokers attempt estate planning. Few, in fact, have any knowledge of valid estate planning. Most have no legal or tax training.

Many brokers play upon your desire to save money. They promise to save you, among other things, a probate fee. These salespeople tell you, "If you buy what I sell and take ownership (title) the way I advise, you will avoid probate." Generally you avoid probate only if you give your assets away *now*, while you live, which is preposterous. You know it. I know it. You would never buy what this salesperson is offering if you actually realized what you must do to avoid probate. To avoid probate is to own nothing when you die. The only way to have nothing when you die is to give it away while you live.

One way to lose your assets is through the use of *joint tenancy with right of survivorship*. Most brokers don't understand why or how probate can be delayed if title is taken in joint tenancy. They often don't care or know that this can cause gift taxes, which can greatly exceed any possible probate fee. There is also a tremendous danger that jointly owned assets may be seized by the creditors of your joint owners.

Knowledgeable brokers now realize that there is a danger in joint tenancy but they don't necessarily know why. Some brokers push the purchase of stocks through a "trust" vehicle. This is not a living trust; this is not a real trust. This is usually worse and more dangerous, if possible, than joint tenancy. Frankly, I think it is ridiculous to use a broker for estate planning. If you do, you will probably lose money. You would be well advised to purchase nothing from any broker who tells you that he will save you a probate fee. If he demonstrates in this way that he knows so little about this area, perhaps he has a similarly poor knowledge of the stocks he recommends.

Unfortunately, there are also some attorneys who don't understand estate taxes or the dangers of joint ownership of property. I recently read a publication, allegedly written by an attorney, which attempts to tell the reader how to avoid using a lawyer in all applications of the law. The book states that you should avoid probate at all costs. The method suggested is joint tenancy with children. It is regrettable that some attorneys abdicate their professional responsibilities by giving advice in areas of the law in which they themselves have such limited knowledge.

Many retired people will lose assets by following the advice of "experts" who are generally unqualified to discuss entitlement-how to own things. Remember, the burden is on you: Get proper advice from a knowledgeable source. Recognize the limitations of brokers and mutual-fund salespeople; their educational backgrounds do not usually equip them to give legal advice on how you should own or take title to investments.

## Don't Abuse Your Assets

Fear of mishandling their assets causes many people to liquidate holdings upon retirement. This money is then placed in a variety of savings accounts. Banks and savings institutions enthusiastically encourage this. Question their motivation: It is simply profit, and the profit is not yours!

Perhaps you think this is "security." It is in fact the exact opposite. You believe all these accounts are insured, and this impresses you. Not all such accounts are 100 percent insured for you. There can be a limit on the amount of insurance that any individual can receive, regardless of the number of different joint accounts he or she may open in any financial institution, including all branch banks. But even if your assets are covered by insurance, why protect your money at the expense of shrinking these assets?

Savings institutions in my community have opened "Private Executive Clubs." These can only be described as a "come on." For example, if you put $5,000 or more into a savings account at these institutions, they grant you membership privileges such as:

1. The right to sit there all day during banking hours and read a variety of magazines

2. The right to make one long-distance telephone call a month without charge

3. All the free coffee (generally quite weak) you can drink

4. Some alleged group-travel benefits

So what you're really receiving is the most expensive cup of coffee imaginable and the most expensive telephone conversation in the history of AT&T. The unwisdom of keeping large amounts of your assets in nongrowth accounts at savings institutions can be illustrated by the choice made by a well-informed retired top executive from a large savings institution whom I represented. He was a very wealthy man, but he did not keep more than $5,000 at any time in any savings account anywhere.

Most savings and loan institutions and most commercial banks offer a variety of savings accounts. These institutions particularly push their time certificates of deposit, which allow them to hold your money for a longer time. The average savings account pays interest between 5 percent and 7 percent per year. The average time certificate of deposit pays interest from 6 percent to 8 percent, but you must leave your money with the institution for a considerable period of time.

Today inflation shrinks your money at a distressing rate. For the month in which I am writing this chapter, hard inflation is $7\frac{1}{2}$ percent. We all hope that inflation will not continue at this high rate, but we can anticipate a minimum rate of 6 percent, and there certainly will be times when it will be much higher, even as much as 9 percent. Many economists feel that a small rate of inflation is a necessary incentive to growth. In any event, it is here to stay and is likely to increase yearly.

Current inflation means that the buying power of your dollar shrinks at a minimum of 5 percent a year, if we can knock inflation down to that 5 percent level. If the buying power of your dollar shrinks at the rate of 5 percent a year, and you keep assets in a nongrowth investment (such as a savings account), you will really earn, in actual buying power, 5 percent less than the interest you receive. Thus if your bank account pays 5 percent, in reality you earn nothing because the buying power of your money has decreased by 5 percent in that year. In fact, you actually lose money, because the buying power of your principal also depreciates. Thus any money you placed in this financial trap is worth less every day because a savings account does not grow to hedge against inflation.

Inflation is quite simple to understand. If you put $10,000 into one of these financial institutions in any of their interest-bearing schemes, the principal amount of $10,000 always remains at $10,000. There is no possibility of principal growth. Let's assume that you receive the above-average interest of 5 percent from your bank. This produces an income of $500 a year. Assume further that you are at the minimum income-tax level, and only 20 percent is taken for taxes. This leaves you the grand total of $400 in spendable income: only 4 percent on the $10,000. However, if the annual inflation approximates 5 percent, in reality your $10,000 is worth less, or $9,500; therefore, you actually lost $100 each year that you received a net income of $400 after taxes, because your $10,000 today will only buy what $9,500 would have bought when you first deposited your money in that bank. Of course, your loss is much more critical if inflation is higher. In a period when the 9 ½ percent figure is reached, your loss is almost double.

Look at it another way: Today $10,000 might allow you to buy two fully equipped automobiles in the minimum price range. However, five years ago these automobiles would have cost $3,500 each, or a total of $7,000. It is safe to assume that five years from now the identical automobiles will cost somewhere in the area of $6,500 to $7,000 each, so if you leave your money in these financial institutions for five years, your $10,000 will buy you not two minimum-priced cars but one

minimum-priced car and a tricycle. You might however be lucky enough to purchase two compacts. The
same principle applies in the purchase of food.

Inflation depreciates the value of your dollar day by
day, year after year. You must therefore put your
assets into a secure investment that pays fair dividends
and still allows your principal to increase conservative-
ly and slowly, but enough to hedge against inflation.
Fixed investments do not do this. Life insurance does
not. Annuities do not. Many bonds do not. Savings
accounts do not.

You must be quite wealthy to afford the luxury of
investments that do not increase the principal value.
That is why I repeat throughout this book that *you must
ensure maximum income* and *see to it that both income and
principal retain their buying power*. In other words, you
must hedge against inflation. This is another reason to
consider seriously the purchase of safe, secure, income-producing investments or certain bonds that can
pay sufficient income to hedge against inflation over
any given five-year period by increasing in market
value enough to offset the rise in the cost of living
through inflation.

It goes without saying that I do not believe any
retired person should purchase tax-free bonds unless
he or she has an income in excess of $20,000. The
average retired individual is not at an income-tax level
that justifies the loss of all growth potential with the
purchase of these bonds.

You might think that the security of insured bank
accounts is worthwhile. However, $20,000 in a savings
institution will probably be worth only $16,000 in real

buying power in five years. This becomes critical when you consider the cost of food. Even beer will be too expensive for you as inflation constantly minimizes the real buying power of your dollars. Five years from now, with your principal thus invested, you will be unable to maintain your present standard of living.

It is undeniably prudent to have some cash savings for emergencies. It is, however, absurd to place all your assets in a financial institution that offers nothing but an inflation trap. The advertisements tell you about daily interest; they don't mention the daily shrinkage of your principal. You must realize that both exist.

The average middle-class retired person arrives at his Shangri-la with a pocketful of cash. Many financial institutions conduct active, aggressive campaigns to get their hands on this money. They can be quite creative in this endeavor. Sometimes their methods are manifestly preposterous and morally outrageous. They bombard you with inducements to place all your money in their hands, then they pay you what amounts to approximately 1 to 2 percent income in real buying power after income tax and the shrinkage from inflation are deducted. All the free coffee in the world hardly makes this abuse worthwhile.

If you are enamored of your favorite financial institution, you would be better advised to buy its stock. You will be ahead of your neighbor who simply puts all his or her money into the institution's savings plans.

Check the insurance company that insures your savings bank (and your accounts) very carefully. Be sure it has assets of value behind it. Most banks and savings institutions are insured, but not all financial institutions have Federal Deposit Insurance Corporation or Federal Savings and Loan Insurance Corporation protection. There are some financial institutions that insure themselves with private insurance companies, a fact that should give you pause. Why can't they insure with the appropriate federal insurance corporation? Is it perhaps because they cannot qualify for this insurance? Are they doing something wrong? It's bad enough that any of these institutions guarantees a loss in buying power, without risking the loss of all your money at once.

Sometimes the corporations that insure bank accounts and savings accounts are owned by the stockholders or directors of the very same bank or savings institution. In many communities anyone can buy an old insurance charter not presently in use. In these communities a bond as low as $250,000 filed with the Insurance Commission is all that is necessary to form a valid insurance company. It's quite possible that some companies have few assets beyond that $250,000 cash bond.

There are some financial institutions with millions of dollars in savings accounts insured only by this $250,000 cash bond. If that savings institution goes broke, only the first $250,000 worth of claims will be protected and paid. This is a grotesque situation. It is even more grotesque because the insurance commissioners do nothing to correct these abuses. Once you have lost your money, it does you no good to question whether these insurance commissioners exist to protect you or to protect the insurance companies. *You* must protect *yourself* by investigating in advance. You have a duty to yourself to be sure that the insurance company that insures your account has sufficient assets. You are retired. You have the time. Check around.

Remember, too, that any investment and any savings institution that offers you interest well above the average may be carrying a risk factor. It is not wise for you to assume any unnecessary risks once you retire.

Even financial institutions with the appropriate federal insurance can only insure one individual's account in that bank up to $40,000. In order to grab more of your money, these institutions have invented a variety of ways for you to open different accounts. Most of these peculiar accounts may place you in severe financial danger. In my state, for example, some salespeople who handle new accounts for the banks and savings institutions urge you to open the account in your name, with your spouse as joint tenant. They will also urge you to open an account with your child's name on the account. In addition, they urge you to open yet another account with you and your spouse each acting as trustee for the other. They also advise additional accounts wherein you act as trustee for your children. And so on. Unfortunately, very few of these salespeople understand the legal complications of entitlement.

If you were told repeatedly by experts that something you were doing was wrong or immoral, would it not give you pause? If you were also informed that there were serious dangers in what you were doing, wouldn't you also ask, "Why?" If you were a salesperson and were told that the advice you were giving those who use your services was not only incorrect but also dangerous, wouldn't you attempt to learn more?

Oddly enough, those salespeople who are hired to sell different savings accounts do not care to thus educate themselves. They are generally more interested in winning a free weekend at a resort for selling a certain number of savings accounts in any given monthly period. The financial institutions do not train their sales staffs to understand the legal significance of the accounts they promote. My colleagues and I have pleaded with sales personnel at banks and savings institutions not to recklessly advise the use of joint tenancy. We further call attention to the danger when a bank account is opened in your name as trustee for another person. Nevertheless, these financial institutions want your money so desperately that they ignore the dangers and allow members of their staffs to practice law without a license—and, more important, without the proper education. *You* suffer the consequences.

Their rationale seems to be that joint tenancy eliminates probate. It does not; it merely *delays* probate, and tax consequences can actually cost more than probate. Moreover, you can lose these accounts to the creditors of your joint owner.

Once you are aware that the primary motivation of banks and savings institutions is not to serve you but to make profit for themselves from your money, perhaps you will be more cautious. Let us not blame the banks or the bank clerks or the savings institutions for our own errors. It is human nature to wish to appear more knowledgeable than we are. Everyone likes to give advice. However, you wouldn't go over to a sales clerk in a department store and ask his or her advice on what you should do in a major real estate transaction. You wouldn't ask this person to manage and invest your assets, would you? Why, therefore, would you ask a mere clerk-salesperson at a savings institution what to do with your assets? He or she doesn't understand the complexities of entitlement or ownership of assets. Should you ask an officer in any of these institutions the questions you ask the clerk-salesperson, the officer would probably tell you that he or she is not authorized to practice law and would suggest that you visit an attorney. Banks and savings institutions are in great error for not instructing their clerks to do the same.

When I question these clerks, they say, "We don't advise customers. People insist that everything be in joint tenancy." When I question my clients, they say, "The tellers at the bank get angry if we don't take their advice. They demand that we make everything joint or in trust." You no longer need make this mistake now that you realize that these clerks are not experts and that you follow their advice at your own peril.

In later chapters concerning trusts and joint tenancy, I shall explain some of the dangers in more detail. For now, be aware that you should never have a savings or checking account of any type in anyone's name but your own if you are a single person. If you are married, and it is a *first* marriage and *only* a first marriage, it *might* be safe to consider using a joint-tenancy account. You should never use a joint-tenancy account with a second spouse unless you are willing to risk the possibility that you might disinherit your children. This is explained in detail in Part Six. Joint tenancy can be expensive even for a husband and wife in a first marriage if your estate is taxable, for joint tenancy always increases the tax on a taxable estate. Never, *absolutely never*, put a child's name on anything you own. This is particularly true of bank accounts, stocks, and your home. Should you do this, you might suffer severe gift taxes that greatly exceed any savings on a probate. Worse, you can lose these assets to the creditors of your joint owner, and your death tax can increase if the gift is still taxed back into your estate.

The primary reason that some financial institutions recommend these various accounts is that they realize that you want an insured account, and since no account can be insured beyond a limited amount, they recommend these questionable methods of obtaining and holding onto your assets. Usually they tell you that all of the different savings accounts you own are insured, but often these accounts are not fully insured to you. Let me repeat, for this is important. If you have your name on different savings accounts with different people, while these accounts might be insured under certain circumstances, there is not 100 percent insurance in each instance to both of the joint owners. You are only entitled to a limited amount of insurance for joint accounts.

For example, assume that you placed your daughter's name on your $20,000 savings account; the account now reads "You and your daughter as joint tenants with right of survivorship." The bank subsequently goes broke. (Banks still do this.) In this example, assume that this bank had government insurance, so it will ultimately be paid, but it might take one to two years for you to receive your money. Before the insurance is paid there must be a complete audit of all accounts in that bank and all bank assets. This is yet another reason why you should not have more than one savings account at any one financial institution, even if there is full insurance. Spread your risk so that if the financial institution goes broke you won't tie up all your assets. If you insist upon multiple savings accounts, at least use different banks for each account. In any event, whenever the above account is paid off by the insurance company, you will receive only $10,000. Your daughter will receive the other $10,000. Now I know *your* daughter will give you back that $10,000, but your neighbor's daughter might not—especially since she will be making her parents a gift of the $10,000, on which she might well have to pay gift taxes.

Most financial institutions know insurance monies can be split, yet they give the impression that these additional accounts are fully insured to you. A reasonable person might ask why these financial institutions suggest such accounts. I have never received a direct answer from any financial institution I've questioned on this. The obvious reason is profit; unfortunately, you don't share the profit, and you accept all the risks. Remember these important rules:

1. It is dangerous and can be very expensive to use joint tenancy on any bank account unless you are husband and wife in a first marriage and your total assets will not produce a taxable estate.

2. Never, *absolutely never*, put a bank account in your

name as trustee for someone else. This can be financial suicide.

3. Never put a child's name on any of your assets.

If you do any of these things, there is a chance that you will lose these assets.

It is essential to have a savings account. We must prepare for emergencies. There is, however, a substantial difference between having an emergency savings account and placing all your assets into a variety of savings accounts. These accounts can cause you to lose your money and, if nothing else, can lessen the buying power of your money through inflation. Although I am an enthusiastic believer in reasonable savings accounts, I also believe you should not abuse your assets by putting everything you own into them.

# SUMMARY
# OF
# PART TWO

You can do nothing more cruel to your spouse than to keep him or her uninformed about family financial matters. It is your mutual duty to demand that you both know everything. It is essential that both of you learn how to maintain family records, pay bills, handle investments, and write checks together. Both of you must know your assets, which means both your joint assets and the things you might own individually in your own names. Each of you must know the location of everything and the names of your advisers. It is the duty of all spouses to educate each other. Do not leave your spouse in the dark.

Once you retire, stop speculating with your assets. This does not mean, however, that you should take good assets out of the marketplace and waste them in savings accounts. If the stocks you own are not income-producing, but have greatly increased in value through the years, do not hesitate to sell them. Too many retired people do not sell non-income-producing assets simply because they are afraid of a capital-gains tax. There is reason, because of the Tax Reform Act of 1976, to fear capital-gains taxes. They can be substantial; indeed, they are confiscatory. However, you can minimize the impact of your capital-gains tax if you sell some of your non-income-producing assets as you prepare for retirement during your last working years. Capital-gains taxes still mean that a profit has been made. It might be shortsighted to avoid paying a modest capital-gains tax (if your accountant tells you it *will* be modest) when you can then purchase income-producing investments for your retirement. As a result of the 1976 Tax Reform Act, your heirs will no longer receive a step-up in basis and wipe out the capital-gains tax as a result of your death. Today, your heirs will have to pay some sort of a capital-gains tax once they sell the assets you leave them. It would appear that it is not always advantageous today to hold on to non-income-producing investments in an attempt to save capital-gains taxes, if you can better your position and income while you live.

You must constantly try to obtain the maximum income with maximum security when you retire. It might not make sense to continue holding valuable assets that are not income-producing when you could otherwise own assets that might provide additional income for you.

When you purchase assets after retirement, put them in your name alone, or in your name and the name of your spouse if a *tax-trained* adviser tells you that it is prudent. Remember that you cannot get adequate or proper advice from most stockbrokers about how you should take title. Above all, *never* put a child's name on anything you own.

Don't liquidate all your assets and put them into

savings accounts. It is important and necessary to keep an emergency savings account. Any fully insured savings institution with insurance carried by one of the federal agencies is a good place for this emergency account. It is imprudent, however, to have a number of savings accounts, or more than $10,000 in cash, wasting away in a savings institution. Time certificates of deposit and savings accounts depreciate daily as a result of inflation. If you take all your assets and put them into savings institutions your income in five years might not permit you to eat properly, because in five years inflation would have taken a good 25 percent of the value of your money. Have only *one* emergency savings account, and put the rest of your assets into a secure, conservative, income-producing investment that will protect you and hedge against inflation.

# PART THREE:
## *Wills*

## 9. YOUR PROBATE LAWYER AND YOUR EXECUTOR

A will is never probated. Let me repeat: A will is *never* probated. An *estate* is probated, with or without a will. A will makes the probate less expensive. Generally, it completes the process of passing your assets on to your heirs quickly and efficiently, with minimum costs.

Simply put, your will is your declaration of intent. It is a statement of what you want done with your assets after your death. Anyone who owns anything of value or will inherit something of value should have a will. This is especially true of a husband and wife, who always inherit from each other.

Just think: You spent your time and fortune gathering your assets throughout your lifetime. You always sought the best advice. Now you plan to give these assets away, often without expert advice. Or you plan to dispose of everything in a five-minute conference with a lawyer. You give no proper thought either to what you have or to what you really wish to have done with it. You are transferring the total assets of your life. They certainly deserve some serious consideration. There are many alternatives.

The probate lawyer is an expert in the field of estate planning, which includes the drafting of legal documents such as wills and trusts. He is the logical person to give you advice.

Not making a will is the ultimate irresponsibility, but nothing is more subject to expensive court fights, unnecessary taxes, and abuse of your assets than those mistakes made in "avoiding" probate. It is difficult to understand the current tendency to accept as fact the elaborate nonsense written about this subject without considering either the author's qualifications or his or her motives. All too often life insurance companies present you with pamphlets proclaiming that they can do your estate planning for you—and without charge. This is O.K., so long as you understand their motivation. They are trying to sell you insurance, and are not always capable of estate planning or minimizing your taxes. The stockbroker who tells you how to take title (ownership) is misleading you; so is the real estate broker who tells you he or she can handle your deeds or that you don't need a will if you take title in joint tenancy.

All states acknowledge and allow one common type of will: the *formal will*. It is prepared by your attorney after he interviews you and ascertains what you want. He will also advise you on the most efficient way both to minimize estate and inheritance taxes and to distribute assets to your heirs. The most well-advised among you already have such a will.

Another type, also a written will, is called a *holographic will*. This is a will written entirely in the handwriting of the deceased. Seventeen states* and Puerto Rico allow you to use such a will without any limitations. Twenty-three states† and the District of Columbia do not allow such a will. The remaining states and territories allow such a will under certain specific, unique circumstances. Some of them require that you be out of the United States for one year, or in military service and away from home for one year, and the requirements or forms that apply vary.

A holographic will is at best a tricky and expensive procedure. You would be well advised never to use one. This is particularly true if you live in a state that allows it but only under certain conditions: You had better know these conditions. It is safer to assume that you should not use a holographic will.

If you do decide to write your own will, be sure that it is written entirely in your own handwriting. Date the will above your signature and sign it on the bottom. Make certain nobody else writes anything on the paper. Be sure you do not type or print such a will. It must be written entirely in your hand to be valid in most states. This will should not be witnessed by anyone, unless the state requires witnesses. The fact that it is written entirely in your handwriting will be enough, once your signature and handwriting are established and proven. In those states that require the holo-

---

* Alaska, Arizona, Arkansas, California, Idaho, Louisiana, Mississippi, Montana, Nevada, Oklahoma, Pennsylvania, South Dakota, Tennessee, Texas, Utah, Virginia, and West Virginia.

†Alabama, Colorado, Connecticut, Delaware, Florida, Georgia, Hawaii, Illinois, Indiana, Kansas, Kentucky, Maine, Massachusetts, Michigan, Minnesota, Missouri, Nebraska, New Hampshire, New Mexico, Ohio, Oregon, South Carolina, and Wyoming.

graphic will to be written entirely in your handwriting and without witnesses, anyone else's signature on the will voids it.

My state (Arizona), through its new statute, allows a holographic will to be partially written and partially typed or printed. Those portions which must be in handwriting are the "material" parts of the will. The drafters of this unique statute and the legislators who passed it neglected to define a "material" provision.

The privilege of making a will stems from the Statute of Wills enacted in England in 1540. Before that time various property rights escheated to the state, or specifically to the crown, when the owner died. From 1540 on, various landholders, in return for their services to the king, were allowed to distribute their property first to their oldest male child. After many centuries and family feuds, manipulations, developments, and laws, both in England and the United States, every state now has a statute listing the requirements concerning a will. Since this is a privilege granted to you, and not a right (such as the right of free speech under the Constitution), you must meet the requirements of your particular state statute. If you do not know or cannot understand exactly what that statute says, do not try to prepare your own will.

You do not necessarily save money by writing your own will, and you are apt to make expensive errors. As an estate lawyer, I have seen and, indeed, probated many estates with holographic wills. Every one of these estates cost more to probate than an estate with a formal will prepared by a competent attorney would have. This is a very technical area, and it does not usually make sense to save the very few dollars any competent lawyer would charge for the preparation of a formal will.

Anyone above the age of eighteen can prepare a will or have a will prepared. The person signing the will must have what is known as "testamentary capacity." In other words, he must have the legal ability to make a will. In most states, this means three things:

1. Know what you are doing (making a will)
2. Know what you own (your assets)
3. Know who the law considers to be the natural objects of your property. This usually means your spouse, your children, your mother, or your father. In other words, you must know your exact legal relationship to those relatives (step-, foster, and otherwise) who are one generation before and after you.

The fact that you must have testamentary capacity to make a will does not mean that you must leave your assets to any of these individuals. With the exception of Louisiana, all states and territories that comprise the United States allow you the privilege of doing whatever you want with your assets. Louisiana alone follows the Napoleonic Code, and has what is referred to as "forced heirship," whereby some assets must be left to one's children. The Napoleonic Code, which comes from France, is substantially different from English common law. You will be well advised to visit an attorney in the jurisdiction in which you live if you wish to have a proper will made. There are pitfalls everywhere.

Once you prove that you have testamentary capacity, that there is no undue influence (that nobody, in other words, is twisting your arm or forcing you to make the will), and that you are of sound mind, you can do whatever you wish and leave your assets to whomever you choose.

You can do almost anything you want with a will. Some people use a will during their lifetimes to control their heirs. Others use a will to dispose not only of their assets but also of their ill feelings. I once had a client who wanted his will to read:

> To my former son-in-law, the miserable so-and-so, whom I supported all these years, and who had the complete lack of taste to leave my daughter for that tramp with whom he now lives, heartburn! Heartburn which he should have forever and which I leave him in abundance.

Now this is dangerous. It is also silly. You really should not libel anyone under your will. You may well ask, "Why not?" One clever individual said, "Let them exhume me and sue me." They don't have to. They can sue your estate. They can sue your executor. An estate and an executor can be liable for the torts of the deceased. So try to avoid being nasty in your will.

One person demanded that I put the following clause into his will. I did it because he insisted, and I did not consider it libelous. The paragraph read:

> I leave the sum of $2,000 in trust, for one (1) year [naming a trustee], to be used for a marker for my former son-in-law's grave. Should good fortune dictate that he use it within a year of my death, fine; otherwise this Trust shall terminate, and the assets shall revert to my estate.

It's best to avoid such passions in a will. Just be aware that you should use a will merely to give your property away, not to insult or libel anyone.

Once you decide whom you wish to remember in your will, and approximately in what manner, seriously consider using percentages. For example, if you say, "To my favorite child [niece, or anyone], Martha Swartz, $10,000, and everything else to be divided equally among the rest of my children," you might well have specific amounts in mind for the other heirs. Ten thousand dollars might represent a modest portion of your estate. It might be a large percentage. In any event, if misfortune befalls you and you must spend or lose many of your assets, $10,000 might be an exceptionally large portion of your estate. You might not want such an overwhelmingly large slice of your assets to go to one person. If your estate greatly increases, it would, of course, work the other way. Perhaps you would want Martha to receive more. It would be more prudent of you to say to yourself: "This figure represents 10 percent, or 20 percent, or whatever, of my estate. Therefore, I will give Martha that percentage, rather than $10,000." This percentage will now always remain constant, no matter what happens to your assets. The percentage that Martha will receive, in relation to that of the other heirs, will always be the same. It is therefore much safer to use percentages when you divide up your assets. It will also be easier to handle the administration of your estate, and a more easily handled estate certainly means fewer expenses.

It is possible that your executor will have a choice as to which taxes must be paid. In other words, he might choose to pay capital-gains taxes, income taxes, estate taxes, or any combination of these ultimately to pay the lowest total tax. If you make a specific gift of a specific taxable item such as a stock certificate to a particular person, you force your executor to make that distribution and perhaps lose a good tax-savings opportunity. If you do not name a specific stock for a particular person, but just use percentages when directing gifts out of your estate, your executor will retain all tax options.

It is possible, and worthwhile, to consider listing specific legacies in your will. A specific legacy is a bequest of a particular thing. It is always personal property that has an intrinsic value, such as a family Bible or personal jewelry—things that you want a particular individual to have.

In my law firm, we have drawn in excess of 4,000 wills. Almost every client for whom I have drawn a will has begun by saying something like this: "Oh yes, my family understands that my daughter is to receive my jewelry and the family Bible and my son is to receive the mahogany bed that has been in the family for many centuries." The family might understand this, but unless you state it explicitly in your will, your executor will be obliged to do only what your will says, and a particular heir might not receive his or her specific legacy—unless he or she buys it from your estate.

List all such specific legacies in detail in your will. Prepare a list before visiting your lawyer so that he can incorporate it into the will. It should include your jewelry, any items of unique value, family heirlooms—possessions on which value of any kind can be placed.

Thus you save your family from misunderstandings that could well leave ill feeling after you are gone. Above all, don't leave all your personal assets to one person to distribute among your relatives. It is cruel to put such a burden on any one member of your family. It is your duty to do this yourself. Don't feel that your own children are unique. Daily, clients tell me, "My children will not fight." This is lovely. It is a great, ennobling thought. But if your children are not fighting, and my children are not fighting, who is doing all the fighting?

Never leave cash assets to one individual to distribute to the rest of the family. If one person inherits your money under a will, and the will itself does not expressly state that your money is to be divided (in whatever proportions) among other individuals, this person owns the money. This person has no legal duty to do anything but keep the money. From my own experience, I have found that the child who inherits all the money usually keeps it. Even if you leave all your money to one child because you know for certain that he or she will split it up as you wish among your other children, you almost inevitably cause bad family feelings. Furthermore, you force this one person to waste his or her exemptions and exclusions from taxes. In other words, if one child owns all your assets because you willed them to this child, and that child shares or gives a portion to your other children without any *legal* duty to do this, he or she will be making a gift and will waste his or her exclusions from the Uniform Gift and Estate Tax as a result of the 1976 Tax Reform Act.

Whenever anyone makes a gift, the party who makes the gift must usually pay gift taxes, or use the combined credit from gift and death taxes, if the gift exceeds $3,000 per person in one year. Gift taxes are very tricky. The layperson should not necessarily make gifts without expert advice.

You must remember here that you cannot put the burden on one person, child or friend, to distribute your assets. Not only is it unfair, but if that individual drops dead one hour after you, those assets then belong to that person's estate. They will pass to that person's family or children or whomever that person said should receive his or her estate under his or her own will. You would thereby have disinherited your other intended heirs. If you want your assets to be distributed among different individuals, say so explicitly in your will.

Once you have distributed all your assets in your will, you must name an executor, sometimes called a personal representative. This person, or institution, then has the legal duty to administer your estate. If you don't name an executor in your will, the court will appoint an administrator. The difference between an administrator and an executor is money: An administrator *always* costs more.

An executor simply follows the directions in your will. An executor can be excused, in most instances, from posting bond, if you expressly excuse the bond in your will; otherwise the law requires that an executor post such a bond. An administrator cannot be excused. An administrator must follow the law, regardless of what you say in your will, and he must post that bond. Estate bonds cost 1 percent of the estate per year, a needless waste of money.

I am reluctant to recommend that any client use a human being, other than a spouse, as an executor because human beings become ill, or they can refuse to serve. They can become involved in their own affairs, and estates can drag on. And they can die. Thus, administrators must be appointed by the court to correct the errors of your now unavailable human executor, and bonds must be filed. The disposal of your estate becomes expensive.

It is unfortunate and misleading to blame an efficient probate system for *your* errors in naming executors. If you check carefully into an estate that has allegedly been dragging through court, and which allegedly costs an unreasonable amount of money to probate, in most cases you will find that it was handled by an individual who had no knowledge of what he or she was doing. If you are imprudent enough to name an incompetent executor—one without the education, the experience, the background, or the ability to do the job—you cannot blame the legal system for your own errors. While you live, would you allow this same person to invest your money or tell you what to do with your assets? Why, then, would you let this person handle your estate?

It would be prudent seriously to consider naming a financial institution as your executor. The full-service bank in your community usually has a good, competent trust department. The people there are experts in estate administration. They are efficient, qualified executors. They charge no more than an incompetent nephew would eventually cost. Any executor is usually paid by an award from the court. In my community, executors must charge by the hour and verify their time to the probate court before they are paid. In other communities, executors still charge a percentage of your total estate unless they agree to do otherwise by contract with you. If your relative is named executor, he or she will receive the same award, and in addition usually will hire an accountant, adviser, assistant, and broker, which always increases the costs of probate. Financial institutions offer all these services, except legal services, as your executor, usually for one fee. They usually have the facility, the knowledge, the background, the real estate expertise, and the accountants to do the job correctly. They also have individuals with sufficient business background to preserve and maintain your business if you should leave one. They can sell the business as a valid asset. Too often an incompetent executor unintentionally destroys a family business after the owner dies.

Clients often ask me, "How much money does the state take from my estate?" No money is automatically paid to the state. Your assets would only escheat to the state today if your entire family line were wiped out and you left no will. There would be, therefore, no living children, grandchildren, or other relatives—parents, grandparents, sisters, brothers, nieces. Somehow a relative always manages to "come out of the closet" in situations like this. If you have a living blood relative, your assets will never go to the state.

I am also constantly asked, "Why do I need a will?

Can I not use joint tenancy?" These questions will be answered in Part Six, but for now, be aware that joint tenancy can never replace a will. Everyone should have a will.

The signing of a will is a most serious act. All states recommend a specific method of signing, called "Execution." Generally, two or three witnesses are necessary. The law of the state where you live will define the exact number of witnesses required. The witnesses should watch you sign the will, although they need not read it. In fact, it is not wise to let them read it. Your lawyer will most likely tell you simply to state, "This is my will."

Once you sign the will in front of all witnesses, the witnesses are asked to sign the will in one another's presence and in your presence. This isn't always necessary, but in some states each must sign in front of everyone else. Do this in order to play safe and make sure your will is valid in every state.

Will contests are very expensive. Should you improperly execute (sign) your will, your estate could incur a tremendous loss of assets. You would be well advised to recognize that a will should be prepared only by an expert and executed (signed) under his or her directions.

Finally, once you have your completed will, where should you keep it? A will should not be placed in a safe-deposit box. Most states require your safe-deposit box to be locked immediately upon your death. The box cannot be opened until there is an inventory taken by the state. This takes a substantial amount of time. Your will should be held by your executor. If you name a bank as executor, the bank usually holds the original will without charge in its trust department vaults. This is the safest and most efficient way to protect your will. Should you insist upon naming a relative as executor, then let him or her retain your original will in a safe place. (Be sure to take a receipt for your original will to place in your safe-deposit box.)

Some states might consider your will revoked if you write on the original, formal will after it has been signed. Should you wish to make notes, because you want to change your will or for any other related reason, use a copy. Do *not* mark over an original will, because in many states this automatically revokes the will.

Many good estate planners feel that you should never use a friend or relative to write your will. That person might have a vested interest in who gets what. This is particularly true if you use your in-laws' lawyer. In any event, there are certain basic truths about wills that apply to everyone:

1. Insurance salespersons, bank employees, mutual-fund salespersons, and stockbrokers are usually *not* estate planners. They are commission salespersons. They do not know how to plan estates or draft wills, and they don't work for nothing. You will pay them— only you don't know it. You wouldn't believe how expensive they really are.

2. Everyone should have a will. Certainly each husband and wife has a duty to protect the other and their children.

3. There are no do-it-yourself kits for wills. Estates with homemade wills always cost more to probate.

4. Your will should be written so that if you die tomorrow, what you want to happen will happen. If your wishes should later change, redo your will. A will might not be good forever. If conditions change, so must your will. You see a doctor, dentist, and accountant more than once; perhaps you should check your will at least every five years, if not more often.

5. Do not copy your old will, trying to change it all by yourself. You will make expensive and critical mistakes. Every time two congressmen or two legislators meet for lunch, they change some law. There is no way for you to know if the requirements for doing what you want done have changed. The old patent-medicine man is gone, but the 25¢ will form survives at every stationery store. *Don't use one.*

6. Do not copy your neighbor's will. You do not wear the same size shoes or clothing as your neighbor and you certainly will have different assets, taxes, and possessions to give away. Your family might have different requirements. A will should fit you like a made-to-order suit. No two people are in exactly the same situation. Have your lawyer make your will to fit your needs and wishes and tax requirements. Much of the alleged probate loss will be eliminated if you have your lawyer make a will that fits you.

7. Not every lawyer is qualified to do complicated tax-estate planning. If he is not a tax-trained specialist, he probably has a colleague who is. Ask him to introduce you.

8. Be honest with your lawyer. He cannot draft a proper will for you if you lie to him. Lawyers usually charge on the basis of what they do and the time it

takes. If your lawyer is not aware of your assets, he cannot save you tax money. You might end up with a simple will that could be very expensive to use once you die. Take the time to plan your will carefully.

9. If you enter into a second marriage, be sure to redo your will after the ceremony.

10. Do not plan your will without your spouse's being present throughout the entire process. Each husband and wife must make their needs and wishes known to the other. Each has a right to know what the other is doing. Each has a duty to say if he or she can or cannot live with what the other is doing. Remember: Your beneficiaries must live by what that will says. How would you like to live under the conditions you may be imposing on your spouse?

## 10.  WHAT HAPPENS IF YOU DIE WITHOUT A WILL?

In the time of the common law, the only individuals who could inherit from each other were heirs of the blood. This meant children, parents, brothers, and sisters. If a husband died without a will, he disinherited his wife. If a wife died without a will, she, of course, disinherited her husband. This was very harsh, and state legislatures passed laws to minimize this hardship. They did a rather bad job of it, and in most states if you die without a will, your spouse still gets very poor treatment.

State legislatures passed laws that are entitled "Descent and Distribution or Succession." These statutes direct what happens if you die without a will. Some states allow up to 50 percent of your assets to pass to a spouse and the other 50 percent to be divided among your children. Other states give your spouse only one-third of your property. Still others give your spouse only one-third of your personal property and lifetime use of less than all of your real estate. You or your spouse might therefore find yourself living in a home that is truly owned by a daughter-in-law whom you dislike, if your spouse died without a will. Insist that your spouse adequately protect you and draw a proper will.

As an example, if a spouse dies without a will in my state, the following takes place under our new probate code: All separate property and half the community property belonging to the deceased spouse passes to the surviving spouse. If there is no surviving spouse but there are surviving children who are also the children of the deceased spouse, everything goes to the children in equal shares. If there is a surviving spouse but there are also children surviving the deceased as a result of another marriage, the children of the former marriage will get half the deceased's separate property and a half interest in the community property.

We then have a section in our statute entitled, "Shares of Heirs Other Than Surviving Spouse." Under this statute, if someone dies without a will and there is no surviving spouse, everything will go equally to the children of the deceased. Our statute also says that when there is no will, "children" includes adopted children and children born out of wedlock. It doesn't say that children must have been acknowledged during the lifetime of the deceased. This is an invitation for many people to claim that they are children born out of wedlock, whenever a rich person dies without a will. Furthermore, in my state, if the deceased has no living children his assets go to grandchildren, if any. This often generates a need for the establishment of guardianships for grandchildren who are minors, since minors cannot handle their own affairs. Such guardianships are also very expensive. These are just two examples to show you the absurdity of some statutes on the books, and ours is typical of the equally bad statutes in all states.

Our statute goes on to say what happens if someone dies and has no surviving wife, husband, parent, brothers, or sisters. In such situations cousins and other relatives that you don't know probably inherit your assets.

None of the more than 4,000 clients whose wills we have prepared has been aware of any possible danger. You must obtain your own independent counsel to interpret your state statutes for you, so that you can understand what must be done and how you must protect yourself and your family.

What all such statutes mean, however, is that your property does not escheat to the state any more. Every state has a different law to determine what happens if you die without a will. The percentages are different, but they are all bad. To die without a will leaves a complicated mess that is expensive to straighten out. It is therefore irresponsible not to prepare a will.

In Arizona we have the added issue of community property. *Community property* is those assets that you earn while married and living in a community-property state. Your assets do not automatically become community property if you retire and move to a community-property state later in life. Eight states and Puerto Rico have laws of community property, but the interpretation of the laws in each of these jurisdictions is different. Do not attempt to analyze them yourself; you need the advice of an expert. These laws are another reason why it is foolhardy and dangerous to die without a will.

Some states allow a spouse to ignore the will and take a percentage against the estate regardless of what was specified in the will. These percentages vary from 33⅓ percent to 50 percent. Should you write a will and give your spouse less than she or he could otherwise receive by waiving your will, you invite an expensive lawsuit. Such an act is also guaranteed to cause difficulty among your relatives. This is just another reason for a properly drafted, *formal* will, prepared with valid legal advice.

# 11. YOUR OLD WILL

Clients continually ask if an old will, drawn in another state, is "good" in Arizona. I tell them that it is *valid*, but I doubt that it is *good*. Any will prepared by an attorney and properly executed (signed) often can be valid in any other state if it does not violate some basic law in the state of current residence. However, this does not make it a "good" will. Generally, any will drawn in one state is not good or easy to use in another.

You mean more than "good" when you ask that question. What you probably intend to ask is, "Can that old will, drawn in another state, be used efficiently, inexpensively, and get the job done?" The answer is that your out-of-state will can cause additional and unnecessary expenses to your estate.

Your old will declares that you are a resident of your old state. You might be subjecting your estate to dual-residency (and possible double) taxes. In addition, the witnesses to your old will live in your former state. It is difficult, expensive, and time-consuming to obtain the testimony of these out-of-state witnesses, who are necessary to prove that you had testamentary capacity and that no undue influence forced you to make the will against your wishes. If a witness is still alive, he or she usually must testify at the probate hearing before your will can be admitted to probate, an enormous waste of time and money if the witness must be brought in from another state. The delay and cost to your estate will greatly exceed any legal fee you might pay to prepare a new will in the state where you now reside.

There are other reasons not to rely on that old will. As we have noted, you have no basic *right* to make a will; it is a privilege granted to you by each state. The laws in each state are different, and the requirements are also different. Your previous attorney cannot be expected to know the laws in every other state. Your old will might be subject to attack on many grounds. Don't take such a chance. When you move to a new state, always prepare a new will.

# SUMMARY
# OF
# PART THREE

*Nothing* replaces a will. Life insurance does not replace a will, nor does joint tenancy with right of survivorship. A will is never probated; an *estate* is probated, with or without a will. The will simply makes it cheaper. You save money for your family with a proper will. And you make sure your wishes are followed.

Don't attempt to write your own will. This is a technical task, and you are bound to make mistakes. You are giving away the accumulations of your lifetime, so spend some time and give it serious thought. Obtain the advice of a competent estate-planning attorney who has an understanding and knowledge of gift taxes, estate taxes, inheritance taxes, income taxes, and the laws of the state where you reside. He will save money for you, for your estate, and for your heirs.

It is always expensive to name a layperson without experience as your executor. If you would not let this person direct your market investments, your real estate investments, or control your bank account while you are living, don't let him or her handle the enormous responsibility of clearing your estate after you die. It is always more expensive in the end to use a layperson as an executor.

Preferably, use the trust department of a bank as your executor. The trust department of a full-service bank has experts who know how to handle your estate quickly, efficiently, and inexpensively.

Above all, *don't die without a will*. Most inheritances must go through the bloodline unless there is a will that says otherwise. Husbands and wives are not heirs of the blood. If you want to protect your wife or husband, say so in a will. All states have statutes that allow a little piece of your assets to pass to your spouse if you die without a will, but this little piece is not enough. Moreover, it is always expensive to administer an estate without a will. Wills save money. How much they save depends on how intelligently the will is prepared. Make a formal will with expert help; name the trust department of your full-service bank or a trust company as executor, and your estate should not be abused. There is no better way to guarantee fast, efficient, expert handling of your estate.

Your will could become expensive to use if it is more than five years old, so review it at least every five years to keep it current. That old will, if prepared in a different state than the one in which you now reside, can probably be used in your new state, but will often be more expensive to use and could violate the new state's law or, perhaps, mean something quite different in your new state. Always prepare a new will, with proper legal help, when you move to a new state.

If your present will was signed prior to January 1, 1977, the new tax law might have changed the meaning of portions of it. It will be essential that you revisit your attorney and check your old will carefully to see if the new tax laws require a change to be made in it.

# PART FOUR
# *Probate*

# 12.  WHAT IS
      PROBATE?

Almost every day someone walks into my office and tells me that he wants to avoid probate. When I ask if he knows what probate is, he says, "No." When I ask if he can afford to avoid probate, he doesn't know.

Bad advice in estate planning can make probate costly, just as can bad advice on avoiding probate. The important thing is to have expert legal advice for your own situation.

*Probate* is the orderly passing of assets through court to your heirs according to the terms of a will. If you don't have a will, it is the orderly passing of assets through court according to the terms of your state's statute on descent and distribution. There is *no law* that requires a probate. If you own nothing when you die, there is no probate whatsoever.

The way to avoid probate, and the *only* way to avoid probate, is to divest yourself of your assets while you live. In other words, to avoid probate you must give away everything you now own. And if done improperly, this can be very expensive and dangerous.

Probate guarantees that the people you *want* to inherit your assets will receive them in the least expensive manner, with minimum taxes, commissions, and fees. Should you recklessly adopt some of the side-door conveniences offered to the American public today in any attempt to avoid probate you might do *yourself* serious harm.

Before we discuss when and how you should try to avoid probate, we must eliminate unwholesome, unnecessary, and foolish fears caused by failure to understand the reasons for probate.

People with assets use probate. The reasons are many. Few children know how to dispose of a parent's assets without family fights and misunderstandings. There are, of course, other basic reasons, such as enormous tax complications when you improperly avoid probate; moreover, people with assets generally *cannot* avoid probate safely. Probate-avoidance schemes will perhaps delay probate if a husband or wife dies—until the surviving spouse dies. At that point, however, it is usually necessary to probate. If you take time to plan your estate properly, probate is *not* expensive; it can even save your estate money, especially in taxes.

Today, tax considerations are bigger problems than probate, although probate can be quite costly if you do not plan properly or if you listen to clerks and commission salespeople rather than seeking competent professional help in making estate-planning decisions. The majority of husbands and wives in first marriages will be able to delay probate with proper legal counsel. However, these decisions should not be made by a layperson. Find an expert and get help. You can assume that if the person who offers you advice does not charge you for it, the advice might be dangerous or of limited value. You cannot afford free advice, particularly that given by commissioned salespeople.

*No one* should attempt to avoid probate, regardless of their net worth, except a husband and wife who are both in a *first* marriage. In no other situation can probate be avoided without extreme hazard. If you have a second marriage and use joint tenancy with your second spouse in order to avoid probate, you will suffer gift taxes and will automatically disinherit your children, because you would have given your new spouse a gift of your assets when you made them into joint tenancy, and you cannot give away jointly owned assets by will. Jointly owned property, by definition, means that each of the joint tenants owns it all and the first one to die loses the right to will any of it away. It belongs to the surviving joint owner. If you attempt to use joint tenancy to avoid probate, gift taxes can exceed a probate fee; you also take the risk that creditors of your joint owner will take the property away from you while you live.

At death, all estates can be subject to a United States federal estate tax. There are credits from the death tax, but these are combined with the credits from gift taxes for gifts you make during your life. If you place something into joint tenancy with your spouse or child, you might unintentionally and imprudently have used up the total unified credits you will have, and all of your estate will be taxable at your death. Whether you can safely make gifts that will exceed $3,000 per person in any given year depends on many circumstances. Whether it is worthwhile to use your unified tax credits one way over another will also depend on a number of decisions that you usually will not be able to make without expert advice.

The 1976 Tax Reform Act is a complicated, technical, confused, and confusing law. At the time this book is being written, a technical amendments act is already in process. In other words, those who drafted the bill were apparently confused themselves and a second bill, explaining what they intended to do the first time, must be passed. No doubt there will be many such technical amendments, for the act itself is a questionable piece of leglislation. But it is the law you must live by and it is the law that will determine what taxes your estate will pay the federal government at your death. This tax to the federal government is in addition to any state estate taxes or state inheritance taxes that must be paid. The one sure thing is that it is no longer safe or prudent to indulge in self-help or, worse, take the advice of salespeople relating to estate planning and probate avoidance.

# 13. HOW PROBATE WORKS

Your executor must see to it that proper legal petitions for probate are prepared and that a hearing day in court is set. He or she must go to court with the attorney and explain his or her qualifications. The legal requirements for this are technical.

Timely notices and publications are always necessary. After the hearing, an executor must then proceed to collect assets, prepare inventories, file proper timely legal notice to creditors, prosecute and defend claims, make accountings, collect your assets, sell your assets, pay your bills, pay taxes, obtain tax waivers, make court appearances for permission to do various things, and ultimately prepare a final accounting. The following is a partial list of an executor's duties and an explanation of how an estate is handled. It should be clear that it is far too complicated a process for a spouse, son, or daughter to handle unless they are knowledgeable in this field.

1. An executor must *examine the will and note any special instructions*. If there are no heirs living close by, the executor might also make the funeral arrangements. The executor should then confer with the at-

torney who drew the will (if the will was so drawn) and with members of the family.

2. The next job of the executor is to *safeguard the assets of the deceased and take whatever protective measures are necessary*, even before his or her appointment in court as executor. This can be a very vital period. There are assets that might be wasting, that might perish, or that might disappear if they are not properly protected.

3. *If a business is involved*, the executor must *see to the continuation of the business*, so that the business can either pass to your heirs or be sold in the administration of the estate for top dollar.

4. The executor must *offer the will for probate to the appropriate probate court*. He or she must retain the services of an attorney to prepare and file the necessary petitions, and set a hearing date in court.

5. The executor usually has a duty to *publish a public notice in a newspaper of general circulation that an estate is going to be opened and a will offered for probate* (an administrator will be appointed where there is no will). Legal notices say when and where the court hearing will take place and invite all those who are interested, or who wish to oppose the appointment of the executor or administrator, to come to court.

6. The executor must often *be present in court at the hearing and explain his or her qualifications to the judge*. This is a very important safeguard. The judge will then either appoint the executor or appoint an administrator. Once appointed, the executor takes over the active job of administering the estate. Should the executor become ill or die, the court would then, after

another expensive legal proceeding, appoint an administrator. This is but one more reason why one human being should not be the executor. It is always safer to use the impartial expert—the trust department of a bank, or a trust company.

7. The executor must *publish notice to creditors* after his or her appointment as executor. All states have different time notices and different laws for how long a notice to creditors must run. It is necessary that notice to creditors be published in order to protect the business interests in the community. Many people have obligations that must be paid even after their death. If the executor does not publish proper notice to creditors, the estate cannot close and lawsuits can develop that can be very expensive. Amateur executors cannot be expected to handle such problems inexpensively.

8. The executor must *make an inventory of all the estate's assets*: Collect all cash in the name of the estate; inventory all personal items that might have unique value; collect life insurance payable to the estate or assist the beneficiary named in the policy to collect the insurance; arrange for the supervision and management of any business interests; obtain custody of securities; collect interest and dividends; review leases; prosecute and defend claims; check taxes and loans on any real estate and arrange for the management of properties.

All assets that are owned in a joint relationship with relatives and friends must also be inventoried for tax purposes. Children often hide these assets or refuse to cooperate with an executor, and this makes the probate much more expensive. This is but another reason why joint assets (joint tenancy) should not be used with children.

9. The executor will *appraise all assets for federal estate-tax purposes and/or for the tax requirements of the state where the probate is administered*. Obtaining the proper value of various holdings can be an exhausting and expensive affair. All assets are valued as of the date of death and again, perhaps six months later, for more favorable tax advantages. Low values might offer estate-tax savings, but high values might produce income-tax savings. Again, this is no place for an amateur. The federal estate-tax return must include all assets owned by the deceased, whether or not they are in the probatable estate. For example, assets owned by a deceased person—such as life insurance, joint-tenancy assets, and part of the community property—will often pass outside of the probate. The executor has the duty to evaluate and appraise these assets along with estate assets in preparing the federal and state estate-tax returns. The executor is personally responsible for the payment of estate taxes and all state inheritance taxes.

10. The executor must *continue to administer the estate* governed by the provisions of the will and the law of the last state of residence. (If there is no will, the administrator must follow that state's law for administrations; this is an additional complication and once again, no place for an amateur.) The executor (or the administrator) must give attention to business interests and determine the policy of continuance, liquidation, or sale with due regard to the wishes of the deceased, while considering the wishes of the family and the

family's needs. It takes an individual with great expertise to make correct decisions.

The executor must also review the assets and cash requirements for administrative costs, taxes, and the like. If the estate is nonliquid, the executor must decide which assets shall be sold for immediate funds. He or she must decide if real estate is to be sold, obtain the proper asking price, and make the correct sales arrangements. If no sale is necessary, the executor must attend to the production of the highest possible income from this real estate and negotiate leases. The executor must determine and investigate all claims of creditors. The claims must either be approved or rejected, and there are certain specific legal requirements for the manner of these acceptances or rejections. Any errors made in this area can be expensive. The executor must then present to the court the claims he or she accepts for approval before payment.

11. The executor must now *determine and settle taxes*. This is a highly complicated and technical procedure. It involves numerous options that may be used to reduce both income and estate taxes. Estates pay income taxes just as a living individual does. There are options for reporting income. In some cases the income should be reported by the estate; in other cases it is advantageous to report the income in the tax return of the deceased for the year during which he or she died. These choices require a great amount of knowledge and expertise.

The executor must file income-tax returns for income received in that part of the year prior to your death. Other income-tax returns, known as "fiduciary returns," must also be filed for the balance of the year in which you die and your estate is opened. The executor must review all returns and assist in their preparation. In the estate-tax area, the executor must file timely notices in both the federal and state tax departments. Improper filing can provoke payment of penalties and interest. He or she must then prepare and file the estate-tax return. Obviously, the services of an expert will be required in most instances. Only a competent executor will know where to get proper advice. Remember, the executor is personally responsible for any errors he or she makes.

12. After all the foregoing has been completed, the executor must *prepare the final accounting*. This consists of a detailed statement of receipts and disbursements that will be presented to the court. A date must be set for another hearing, proper petitions must be filed, and notices of such hearing must be made available to all who are entitled to such notice. Errors made at this point are expensive. A layperson usually cannot prepare a proper accounting. He or she certainly cannot prepare an accounting in the manner that will be most inexpensive and advantageous to your estate.

13. After court approval, the executor must *distribute the estate*. Once again, this requires an impartial expert. A supplemental accounting to the court and filing of receipts from the beneficiaries will be necessary. At that time, a final discharge of the executor or administrator can be obtained from the court.

In my jurisdiction, all this can usually be done in six months. If an estate is taxable, the federal government can audit the estate and this might delay the closing. If there is a taxable estate, there are options that an expert may exercise. Assets can be valued at two different times, and there are disadvantages and advantages in choosing one valuation date over another. These taxes cannot be ignored by avoiding probate. If you eliminate probate because you have given away your assets through one of the various methods of avoiding probate, tax returns must still be filed. And this can be a real mess!

A blanket statement that you should do one thing or another, without explaining some of the pitfalls that can result, is as dangerous as straightout inaccurate advice. *You must learn to protect yourself.* Anytime you read a statement that says that everyone should categorically take one action or another, without proper explanation, you must be very careful. Not everyone should probate, but not everyone—most assuredly—can afford to avoid probate. Inaccurate information on this subject that does not explain the dangers in joint property or the problems relating to probate avoidance can cause many people serious distress. You must exercise extreme caution and get your own legal advice from your own attorney if you are to "avoid" probate safely.

One dangerous area usually ignored by those who tell you to avoid probate is estate taxation. Your estate will be taxable and subject to a United States federal estate tax if everything you own exceeds the value of your present credits. By "everything," I mean all real estate, wherever it is located; stocks; bonds; investments; checking accounts; savings accounts; time certificates of deposit; personal property; automobiles;

jewelry; and, more often than not, the full value of your life insurance. Life insurance, as we have previously discussed, can be removed from your taxable estate, but only with the help of an expert.

If your estate is less than your present credits and you are in a first marriage, it might be both possible and cheaper for you to avoid probate through joint tenancy. The tax you will pay in these circumstances does not usually justify using probate simply to avoid taxes. It may be much more convenient to pay a modest tax.

If your estate is more than your present credits, other considerations apply. The federal estate tax is a progressive tax, which means that the more money you have, the higher the tax percentage you must pay. Over your present credits, your taxes begin greatly to exceed any conceivable probate fee.

If you abuse your estate by naming an incompetent executor, or if you name someone who does not have the time to handle the job properly, enormous sums of money can be wasted. This waste is usually inadvertent but it nevertheless occurs. And the inability of *your* executor to administer *your* estate inexpensively is *your* fault!

# 14. THE EXECUTOR

Today, it is quite essential that you have a knowledgeable executor, (sometimes called a personal representative). The Tax Reform Act made substantial changes in income taxes, capital-gains taxes, gift taxes, and estate taxes. A tax-trained, competent executor will be in a position to analyze the tax and which combination of exemptions can be used to minimize your overall tax picture. Executors are now personally liable for any mistakes. You might cause your unknowledgeable but well-meaning relative to defend his or her actions in court when you name him or her as executor. A layperson, even your child, rarely has the tools and resources to make critical decisions. It might be a serious mistake to name even a trusted relative as your executor. It is certainly not the fault of what is normally an efficient, effective legal process if you complicate it by intentionally naming an executor without knowledge or experience.

Probate is one area where you cannot afford to bypass an expert. And it is always cheaper in the end to have an expert, like a trust company or a trust department of a full-service bank or your attorney, handle your estate. If you have no faith in your attorney, he or she should not be your attorney. If you don't have any faith in the trust department of your bank, you should not be doing business with that bank. Consider the tremendous savings for your heirs if you wisely and responsibly name a competent executor.

If you name a relative in Boston to administer an estate when you live in Southern California, you can't expect him or her to walk to California to do the job. There will be expensive airplane fares (first-class, most likely), hotel rooms, ground transportation, and living expenses. It is impossible to administer an estate inexpensively long distance. It is a mistake to name an executor who is not a resident in the community where you live.

An Arizona law was recently passed that says that "a nonresident can be the executor in an estate no matter where he lives." In other words, it is no longer necessary in Arizona that an executor for a resident of Arizona also reside in the state of Arizona. Many of my clients have since rushed back to my office. They are delighted. They say, "We can now name our own dear child to handle the administration of our estate." This always appalls me. I ask them whether they understand what an executor must do. They don't. I ask them if they know anything about the availability of their relative when they die. They don't. Their standard answer is, "Oh, he'll [or she'll] be glad to do it for me."

Unfortunately, you can't run your business in one state while you live in another unless it is large enough to have expert managers. Your executor cannot handle your estate inexpensively from another jurisdiction. The executor must do all the things previously mentioned. They must be done in the state in which you last resided. The court appearances in the state where you last lived will require that your executor and his attorney be there. In other words, a nonresident executor might go back and forth three or four times in order to get the job done properly, and will demand that all expenses be paid because he or she was obliged to come in and administer your estate. Just think of the expense! Your executor may come out here, stay at the best hotels, have a wonderful vacation, and bill it all to your estate. It has happened more than once.

My partner was once presented bills exceeding $2,300 by the executors of an estate. They came out to Arizona with their families and had a wonderful vacation. Among other things, they stayed at one of our top resort hotels and ate extremely well. I refused to present these bills to the court. They are upset, but they are not nearly as upset as the other heirs would be had I accepted such bills. Your remaining heirs demand that the fun and frolic of your executor not be paid for by your estate. Name an executor who is a resident of the state where you reside. Anything else must, by its very nature, be too expensive.

Finally, it has been my experience that quite often an out-of-state executor simply renounces the appointment and refuses to serve because he or she cannot afford the time away from business and family. When that happens, the court must appoint an administrator, and that is always a more expensive route to take.

## 15.  THE COST
##        OF
##        PROBATE

Probate need not be expensive. Generally, you set the cost with your own estate planning. In my state, executors' fees are based on an hourly wage. The executor must keep time records and prove his or her time to the probate court before requesting a fee. In many states the executor does not share your assets through the use of a commission. More states will be passing laws that will require executors to keep time sheets and charge by the hour. Those states that still allow commissions to executors do not *require* that executors receive a commission. You can agree in advance with your executor that there will be an hourly fee. Draft your will to indicate that your executor is to work on an hourly basis (it makes sense to negotiate with your executor before preparing the will). It would seem prudent to spend a little time and a few dollars to have a proper estate plan and a valid will prepared by a competent estate-planning lawyer. You will save your heirs money. If your state allows executors to take a commission, a commission can still be cut to a minimum through proper negotiations.

In addition to the executor's fee, there will always be an attorney's fee. In most instances the attorney's fee will be the same as the executor's. It can, however, be less, and at times it can be more. It is always more when you write your own will or name a person who lives out of state as executor. Such actions always increase the lawyer's workload.

If you want to name a relative as executor merely because you want the personal or family involvement, do so. However, if you name a relative and your attorney (assuming that the attorney is an estate lawyer and knows what he or she is doing) as *co-executors*, enormous savings are available. (The banks, naturally, never tell you about this.) This way, your attorney can do all the work and mail it to your co-executor for approval. In other words, your lawyer co-executor can do nothing without the consent of his or her co-executor, that member of your family. The law requires that *all* co-executors sign and consent to everything. This will relieve your relative from all the difficult work (for which he or she is usually unqualified) and will probably save expensive travel costs.

When you name your lawyer and a relative as co-executors, be sure to state in the will itself that the lawyer must take but *one fee*. He or she must accept the executor's fee *or* the lawyer's fee, but not both. You should also state that your relative will receive *no* fee. This is particularly true if your relative is a beneficiary. If he or she takes a fee, income tax will have to be paid on it, but if he or she inherits it, tax will not have to be paid (unless the state has an inheritance tax). In this way, your estate is expertly handled, your relative is fully involved, and only one fee is being paid. It should be reasonable and not exceed the one statutory executor's fee allowable in the state where you reside.

# SUMMARY
# OF
# PART FOUR

Probate is not an evil. It need not be expensive, either. In fact, it can even save you money. Probate is simply the easiest, most efficient method of transferring your assets from one generation to another or to whomever you name. It is done under the direction and with the approval of a court. Probate prevents your assets from disappearing, your children from fighting, and you from losing your assets in a reckless probate-avoidance situation while you live. It is an efficient system, used by worldly people with reasonable assets.

Only the uninformed attempt to avoid probate without adequate knowledge of what it is. If you question the stories of disasters relating to "probate," you will find in most cases that the executors were generally incompetent. You will *rarely* find that a probate lawyer or the trust department of a full-service bank was an executor in those disastrously handled estates. One exception is that in certain retirement communities, some banks hire undertrained and unqualified people, giving them the title "New Business Developer/ Trust Officer." These individuals, keenly aware of their own lack of competence, recommend clients to certain types of lawyers—their former associates—who have resigned from the trust departments of these country banks to practice law. Sometimes these former bank employee-lawyers are there to protect the inadequately trained trust officers—and this practice is reflected in the cost of your ultimate probate. The executor bank will pay a fee to the probate lawyer and, since most financial institutions hire the lawyer who wrote your will to be the attorney for the probate of your estate, the possibility exists that this old friend might not question the bank's fees as carefully as would an independent attorney who is not beholden to the bank for recommendations or for the existence of a practice. Fortunately, this problem has not reached epidemic proportions, and you can still protect yourself from it by asking the trust officer not to recommend you to a former colleague.

There is no law that requires probate. Indeed, there is no probate if you own nothing when you die. The only way to avoid probate is to give your assets away while you live. But if you prepare a proper will, name a competent executor, and have your affairs in good order when you die, probate will be quick, inexpensive, and will save your heirs some disagreeable arguments.

Probate costs can be reasonable. They only become abusive if you have a bad will or name an incompetent executor. If you want to name a relative as executor for reasons of sentiment, do so and name your attorney as co-executor with your relative. The attorney can do all the work.

Both co-executors must sign all papers. While your

attorney co-executor can do all the work in the state where you live and die, he must always have the consent and approval of your relative co-executor.

If you name a relative and your attorney as co-executors, always state in the will itself that there is to be but one fee and that the lawyer shall receive it. State that your attorney must accept only *one* (executor's *or* lawyer's) fee. In this manner, your estate will not pay a double fee.

# PART FIVE:
## *Trusts*

# 16. THE ANATOMY OF A TRUST

Trusts are not new. They were used in antiquity; in fact, there are records of trusts in the common law as far back as A.D. 1500. There are different kinds of trusts. In this Part, we consider the *living* or *inter vivos trust* and the *testamentary trust*. These are the two trusts that probably most concern the retired. (Savings account and bank account "trusts" are not anything like a true trust. They are a gimmick, as I will explain later.)

It is important that husbands and wives plan all trusts together. Each has a duty to tell the other what he or she is doing and also a right to know what the other is doing. After all, one must live with that trust once the other is dead. If you are the beneficiary, you have the duty to tell your spouse what you want and what your needs are. You must say whether you can live with what is going into that trust. If you haven't done it already, now is the time to do it. Once you are a widow or a widower it is too late to correct omissions.

Much of the wealth in this country is controlled by trusts, since large family fortunes are administered in this way. The trust is an ancient, efficient, effective vehicle in which to handle substantial assets. It is a valid way to minimize taxes. Many competent financial institutions will not take a trust if the assets in trust are less than $100,000 to $500,000. These are the honest financial institutions. They know the expenses involved and don't want to abuse your beneficiary with excessive minimum fees. A trust is *not* cheap, and it can limit free use of property. It is no field for the layperson. Trust forms are more hazardous for the uninitiated than will forms.

A trust must fit your needs and taxable estate carefully and exactly. It must also carefully consider the needs and requirements of your beneficiary. Most new-business trust salespeople who sell nothing but trusts rarely go into the changing needs of your beneficiary. Banks in areas where there are many retired people hire "new-business salesmen" to go after new trust accounts. Too few of them are lawyers and most of them have no tax background. Very few of them have had any experience with what happens at death, when the beneficiary must *live* with the trust.

A living or inter vivos trust and a testamentary trust are quite similar. The basic difference is that a living trust is activated while you live and a testamentary trust, while similar in other ways, is prepared and established in your will but does not become active until after your death. (Many "new-business salesmen" at banks say they don't "believe" in testamentary trusts. I don't blame them. They don't get paid for their work on testamentary trusts until after the death of the person who establishes it.) A testamentary trust is for the benefit of someone else; you don't make a testamentary trust for yourself. A living trust is usually for your benefit, although it can also be set up for the benefit of someone else. It can also have many beneficiaries, one following another when a former beneficiary dies.

My comments about living trusts in this chapter essentially apply to the testamentary trust as well. Any significant differences between the two will be explained. Later chapters will deal with each in detail.

Generally, a trust relationship is a fiduciary relationship. A *fiduciary* is a person who works with another person's money. A corporation (like a bank) can also be a fiduciary. A stockbroker can be a fiduciary—but don't ever make one your executor or trustee. A fiduciary relationship allows someone to hold, use, and invest your assets for your benefit. In other words, a trustee (a fiduciary) holds the assets of another person and is the legal owner of this property. The trustee, however, holds it for the benefit and use of someone else. Simply put, you give your assets away when you put them in trust.

A trust is a legal contract. You agree to give what you own to the trustee; the trustee agrees to hold it and use it for your benefit or the benefit of someone you name. The trustee is now the owner, but the trustee is not the owner for himself or herself or the financial institution; the trustee is the owner for you, or for whomever you wish to name as beneficiary. Therefore, when someone owns something as a trustee *the trustee cannot use it for his or her own purposes* without committing a crime or breaking the contract. If the trustee dies, the trust assets are not in his or her estate for tax purposes. They do not pass under his or her will. He or she cannot give the trust assets away. If he or she becomes ill, a new trustee will be appointed. You might say that a trustee is the legal owner, but it is less than complete ownership. He or she owns it only for the benefit of the beneficiary, who is the *equitable* or true owner.

To create a living trust, a lengthy legal document should be prepared by a competent lawyer/estate planner. Some financial institutions offer to prepare the trust document for you without charge. This is no bargain, but a disaster bordering on the criminal. The bank will give itself too many powers and you will suffer greatly. When you establish a trust you must be very specific. What you want done must be *carefully* explained and detailed into the trust instrument. If you are vague, expensive lawsuits may result. There is a variety of living and testamentary trusts. In all trusts, the duties and liabilities of the parties should be discussed in detail. You must know what assets you put into trust. The trustee must understand what he or she will own and be expected to do for your benefit. You should both understand what the duties and obligations of the trustee will be. You should both also understand what the rights and duties of the beneficiary will be. The trustee must be paid and occasionally will explain the total costs in advance.

A trust is not a money-saving device, and it is not inexpensive. When you establish a living trust you take something you own and give it to the trustee. The trustee can sell it, manage it, invest it, maintain it, or whatever the case may be. He or she then pays the income and dividends to you if the trust was established for your benefit. The trustee will, of course, do the same things for a different beneficiary if you established the trust for someone else.

The trustee has a personal obligation to the beneficiary which the latter can enforce in court, if necessary. The title to the trust property must be split. In the eyes of the law the trustee holds the empty, legal title; the beneficiary is the owner of the equitable title. Equitable title is the stronger title. This gives any beneficiary the right to force the trustee to do things in his or her behalf as established under the terms and conditions of the written trust agreement. If the trustee fails to do the job for the benefit of the beneficiary, the beneficiary, who owns the equitable title, can go to court and force the trustee either to resign or to do the job properly. This is one reason why you should never allow the bank to prepare your trust instrument for you. The bank certainly will not give you the maximum rights your own lawyer would put into the contract or trust instrument for you. I don't mean to imply that the banks necessarily or deliberately mislead you; it is just that some bank trust officers seem to believe that they deserve more power than they truly need. This is particularly true in certain country trust departments of full-service banks in some retirement communities. Here, too few of the trust officers are attorneys or career trust officers such as you find in private trust companies.

In recent years, the living trust has become the most abused, dissipated, expensive tool in the United States for irresponsible and unknowledgeable financial salespeople. They sell living trusts as means of probate avoidance, hence as a savings device.

A trust, however, does *not* truly save a probate fee. It *replaces* the probate fee with a trustee's fee. The trustee's fee can certainly be more expensive in the long run than the probate fee. On the other hand, economy should not persuade you to avoid a trust if a trust is what you need.

There are many valid reasons for a living trust, among them:

1. You are not incompetent, but just forgetful.

2. You are ill and cannot handle your financial affairs.

3. You need help to care for yourself.

4. Your assets are so complicated and your investments so varied that it is now beyond your ability to handle them.

5. You are retired and don't want to be bothered with playing the market or handling investments.

6. You have a large amount of cash and don't want to waste it by having it shrink in a savings account. You want it invested by an expert.

7. You want your assets to be used for the benefit of a minor child or other unknowledgeable person who does not have the ability or capacity to invest it properly and safely.

8. You seek some of the tax advantages available through trusts.

9. You want to provide security and safety for a spouse if you die.

There are substantially the identical estate-tax advantages in the use of a testamentary trust (a trust under your will) as in a living trust. A living trust might offer some income-tax advantages that a testamentary trust might not.

If you decide that you can afford and will benefit from a living trust or a testamentary trust, always name a trustee in the community where you live. Put a clause into all trusts that the "income beneficiary" can ask the trustee to resign and nominate a trust department in a bank in the community of residence if the beneficiary must move to another city. (No trust that I have ever seen prepared by a bank had this clause in it.)

It is foolhardy to name a trustee in a distant place. I had one Arizona client who prepared a trust naming a New York City bank as trustee. I suggested he change it, but he was convinced that his former lawyer had done the proper thing. He is now dead. The trust is irrevocable and his wife is the unhappy beneficiary. Her long-distance telephone bills are enormous.

For many reasons, you need your trustee close at hand. You should be able to go to your trust administrator quickly and bang on his or her desk if you are unhappy. You or your spouse should be able to look him or her in the eye at any time and say, "Okay, tell me why . . ."

It takes a Ph.D. in algebra to understand some of the quarterly computer printouts used by banks. A beneficiary will want to have them explained. There may be many other problems that require personal communication. It is unrealistic to imagine that your beneficiary can receive the same service from a long-distance trustee that a local trustee can provide.

# 17. THE INTER VIVOS OR LIVING TRUST

The inter vivos or living trust is a trust in which you transfer your assets to a financial institution that you name as trustee. The trustee will invest, manage, hold, protect, and distribute your assets. The financial institution will pay your bills, give you the income accruing, and generally make your retirement comfortable. I refer to the trustee as a financial institution because I am of the opinion that only an honest financial institution should be your trustee. Most living trusts are revocable. You can end them or take out any amount of money at any time. In my opinion it is reckless to name your offspring as trustee, because they generally know less about the investment of money and the handling of your assets than you do. Also, they often don't have the time to give the trust the attention it needs.

The usual advantage many seek in a living trust is that their assets will be invested by a group of experts. If you're fortunate, these investments will hedge against inflation. You will thus have a secure retirement and not dissipate your assets unnecessarily. In addition, you would want the money to be spent for your benefit if this should become necessary. I have had occasion to be disappointed in the very slow manner in which some son or daughter trustees invade principal for the benefit of their parents, who are the sole beneficiaries of their own living trusts. In order to guarantee that you receive all your living trust benefits, you should name an expert as trustee. A trust company or the trust department at an honest financial institution is where this expert may be found.

All trustees will be paid. Banks, just as any other business, are profit oriented. They do not work for nothing, and their services do not come cheaply. There is an annual fee; a minimum fee; a withdrawal fee; and a termination fee at death. However, the fees are a bargain if you do in fact need a living trust.

Unfortunately, some trust department new-business salespeople are so anxious to receive your money and put it into a trust that they neglect to draw a proper distinction between those who can afford a trust and those who cannot.

There are also attorneys so anxious to earn a fee drafting trusts—and so anxious to avoid offending the bank that sends them trust business—that they don't accurately analyze the cost features for you. You have to protect yourself by not automatically going to the attorney recommended by the trust department in a bank in a retirement community. In many retirement communities former trust officers resign and set up law offices around the corner from their former employer bank. The bank recommends only former trust officers who usually recommend only what the financial institution wants. You would be well advised to seek a competent attorney who is not obligated to the financial institution for the success or failure of his practice.

Today, many financial institutions, particularly banks in retirement communities in the United States, earn high profits from living trusts. With such high-profit potential, it is small wonder that the trust departments push trusts without dwelling on the costs to you. The trust departments talk about annual trust fees, which are a percentage of the trust assets. Many trustees charge a yearly percentage of the entire amount of assets in trust. Some charge a higher percentage, but only on the income the trust earns. Trust fees generally approximate something like $8.00 per $1,000, a modest charge for those who need a living trust and comparatively inexpensive for the generally good services they receive. Other financial institutions charge $5.00 per $1,000 in trust but have a minimum annual fee of $500 to $1,000 as a base and charge $5.00 per $1,000 on everything thereafter. In any event, $8.00 per $1,000 based upon everything in the trust can be quite heavy when you compare it with the annual income.

Let's assume that you have $100,000 in trust. Further, let's assume that the annual fee of $8.00 per $1,000 would be $800 a year. Now, assume that you have the extraordinary good fortune of a trust that earns 6 percent annually, so that you accrue income of $6,000 per year. The annual trustee's fee of $800 will be taken out of the $6,000 income. That means you pay 13$\frac{1}{3}$ percent of your income as your trustee's annual fee. If the trust has an annual minimum fee of $1,000 per year, this means you will pay 16.66 percent of your income to the trustee as an annual fee. These figures are not explained to discourage you from using a trust. There are many outstanding advantages to a trust, if you can afford one. Your need for a trust should be determined by you with the help of your own independent attorney.

Most trust departments charge you 1 percent for any monies you take out of trust. Regrettably, very few new-business salespeople in trust departments mention this withdrawal fee. In other words, if you invade the principal and take back any of the monies you placed in trust, there may be a 1 percent charge. There is also a 1 percent termination fee when the trust is terminated or at your death. However, trust fees are varied and negotiable and you should always bargain.

It should now be obvious that a trust does not truly "save" a probate fee. It replaces one probate fee after you die with a yearly trustee's fee. Over the years, the annual trustee's fee should add up to more than a probate fee. It is for this reason that I say a living trust should *never* be used simply to "avoid" probate, if there is no other valid reason for the trust.

This discussion on the cost of trusts is not intended to discourage you. If you need a trust, there is nothing that replaces it, and furthermore, some trust institutions have a better than average performance record. They might increase the principal of your assets in trust 2 or 3 percent a year in addition to the other income benefits. If you have any of the many valid reasons for this vehicle, then you can get the added benefit of no probate. However, no probate should be considered only an incidental benefit of the trust.

I am an enthusiastic supporter and user of the living trust. I recommend it to the vast majority of my clients who have sufficient assets and a need for a living trust. However, all trust departments have a minimum fee, which is reasonable and necessary for them to stay in business. Make sure you understand how much you will pay each year, in dollars, and what percentage of your income it equals.

The trust vehicle works quite simply. You transfer your assets to the trustee, who becomes the legal owner. You remain the equitable owner and the trustee must use the assets for your benefit. While you live, you *can* direct the investments. This is called a *directed living trust*. I don't recommend this to most of my clients, because I believe that the retired and people of advanced age have no business being in the marketplace. I certainly don't believe that most widows should be playing around in the market. If you are going to have a living trust, take advantage of the expertise in the trust department of your trust company or bank. Let them handle the investments.

Another abused area: Most trust departments in large banks have a variety of common trust funds that are not unlike mutual funds. They certainly can be a well-run, conservative type of investment. There is nothing wrong with them. Most people would be in a better position if their assets were there. Nevertheless, the banks make enormous profits on these common trust funds. It should not cost them much more to have $1 million or $10 million in these trust funds. They don't have to work hard for their fee if they keep your assets in these common trust funds. Generally, you still pay a full trust fee whether you are in a common trust fund or whether they handle your trust account as a separate investment fund. A few banks seem to have had an attack of conscience, and recently some of them are starting to charge lower fees for common trust funds.

If you have good securities that provide sufficient income and reasonable growth, there is often no reason to sell them simply in order to put you into a common trust fund, and when they are sold, capital-gains tax must often be paid. Many banks don't inform you of this until after the fact. If you have good investments and set up a living trust, you must direct the trustee bank *not* to sell your assets without your consent, and *not* to place them automatically into a common trust fund.

Every individual who at a certain stage in life or beyond a certain age has substantial assets (and by substantial assets I mean something in excess of $100,000) might benefit from some type of living trust. Exactly when this point is reached can only be determined by your individual circumstances and your physical and emotional stability. If you don't have enough money to generate sufficient income to meet the annual minimum charge of a trust, then it is simply not good economics to have a living trust. Some new business salespeople, in their enthusiasm, do not understand this point.

Assume that you have good, secure investments, blue-chip securities, and that your health is fairly good; there would then seem to be no reason for you to have a living trust. You are, nevertheless, the person who should seriously consider a testamentary trust under your will for the benefit of your spouse or other heir. Many widows inexperienced in money management might feel more secure with a testamentary trust. Once again, this is a matter of economics; you should first consider whether you have sufficient assets to place what you own into a trust for your heirs.

If you have any of the valid reasons for a living trust, then you cannot concern yourself with costs. The price you pay will be a bargain. Your assets will be preserved, and you will be well maintained if you use a full-service trust department at a full-service bank or a trust company as trustee.

You should never have a living trust with a mutual-fund company as trustee. I explain why in great detail in Chapter 23: "The Pseudo-Trust That Is Not a Trust."

It is equally imprudent to have a trust with your relative as trustee. Recently a woman visited me who had established a trust with $120,000 in cash and blue-chip stocks. She had named her son-in-law as trustee. "After all, he was a businessman," she told me. This businessman dissipated the trust; in fact, he destroyed it. He used some of the assets for his own personal affairs and he lost them. He then tried to make spectacular profits in order to replace the money; this reckless speculation caused even more losses, so that ultimately the total assets this woman owned were less than $20,000. She could sue him, but he is her son-in-law. He is also broke.

Don't take such foolish chances. If you need a living trust, use a trust company or the trust department of your full-service bank as trustee. That is where experts will handle your affairs properly. If they commit errors that a reasonably prudent trustee would not commit, they have substantial assets behind them and you can sue and collect damages. If you name an individual as trustee and he or she abuses your money, there is usually no chance to recover your losses. If you want to be safe, never, absolutely *never*, make a living trust with anyone except a trustee in the trust department of your full-service bank or trust company. To do otherwise is often an invitation to disaster.

There are a variety of living trusts. Many individuals with excellent credentials believe that the testamentary trust (Chapter 18) is becoming less useful. However, it still has an important place in estate planning. This is especially true for those who are not completely retired or who want to protect a surviving spouse.

Another type of living trust, which is very popular and practical, is called an *unfunded living trust*. Some people refer to it as a *standby living trust*. This living trust is exactly like any other, except that you will not put anything into this trust now. An unfunded living trust is often funded with life insurance policies on the life of the trustor, so it is actually not truly funded. There is, of course, no annual trustee's charge for such a trust so long as it is unactivated and unfunded. Many individuals will create such a living trust and fund it with $10 or $20 just to put it into existence on the bank's books, awaiting emergencies.

The utility, validity, and appeal of such a trust is

obvious. If you become ill, the trust is there, and you can activate it at once without delay. This is a most efficient and highly recommended estate-planning tool. The security and peace of mind you will enjoy from this kind of trust often remove a lot of worry. Should your assets become a burden to you, simply fund this trust. It is an efficient, fast, and highly recommended trust vehicle.

An unfunded living trust requires that you spend some money today for your protection in the future. Many retired individuals don't like to spend money unnecessarily. On the other hand, this should not stop you from seriously considering an unfunded living trust if you do have assets and you believe that the burden of maintaining them will increase through the years. The obvious advantage of such a trust becomes apparent should you become ill. If you then fund this existing trust and your illness is fatal, your spouse would have the advantage of the living trust already in existence and would not have to wait for the administration of the estate to have the trust funded. I believe any retired person with assets can probably benefit from an unfunded trust.

# 18. THE TESTAMENTARY TRUST

A testamentary trust works almost exactly like a living trust. The basic difference is that you make the trust instrument in and as a part of your will; thus, the trust does not go into effect until after your death. You will not pay an annual trustee's fee while you live. Once you die and your estate is administered, your assets will pass into the trust. The bank will be the trustee and whoever you name will be the beneficiary. At this point, after your estate is closed, the trustee's annual fee will commence.

The testamentary trust is a most underrated vehicle. It should be used more. During my many years of practice in a retirement community, I have seen ample demonstration that many widows benefit from testamentary trusts.

The shock of being alone after a lengthy and happy marriage continues for a long time. Many widows never completely recover. Few of them know how to make investments or how to manage the investments they already own. Nothing is stable in the marketplace— many good stocks this year are next year's losers. You cannot assume that your widow or other beneficiary will necessarily have access to proper advice. In such a case, probably the best thing you can do is to establish a testamentary trust under your will. Your beneficiary can then continue to carry on normal activities without the burden of money management.

Too many of my widowed clients make imprudent, reckless, and absurd investments. One recently actually purchased a mortgage from a scoundrel disguised as a cleric. He told her he was selling secure second mortgages. She took her entire cash savings and purchased a mortgage that was to pay her 16 percent interest a year. She couldn't resist; the income potential was so enormous and he was, "after all," she told me, "a man of the cloth." He wasn't even an honest man, much less a man of the cloth. Nor did he own the real estate on which he allegedly sold the mortgage. She lost everything. This is not a unique case among confused, elderly widows and widowers.

If you establish a testamentary trust under your will for the benefit of your spouse and are careful how it is drafted, everything placed into that trust need not be probated when the spouse dies, and the assets need not be taxed to his or her estate. If the beneficiary of your trust is not a spouse, then the assets placed in trust will usually be added to the total assets owned by that beneficiary, in or out of trust; and when the beneficiary dies, everything will be taxed into the estate of the beneficiary.

The most recent law relating to trust and estate taxation dates from January 1, 1977. It is highly technical, inconsistent, subject to a variety of confusing interpretations, and, in some opinions, painfully abusive. It is no longer prudent or safe to copy any trust form or recopy your old trust or will or allow anyone but a highly trained estate-planning attorney to discuss these instruments with you and prepare them on your behalf. Indeed, people with existing wills and trusts would be well-advised to visit their attorneys immediately to see if the new tax laws substantially change the tax implications of their present estate plan. In many cases the law has drastically affected the taxation of your estate. Contact your attorney for a reexamination of your old will or trust if it is dated before January 1, 1977. One thing is certain in every case: It is no longer prudent or safe for you to copy your old will or trust simply to make a one-sentence change. Renewing an old will or trust might cause you to incur new tax liabilities. It might be more prudent to use an amendment procedure. It is more vital than ever before that you do not indulge in self-estate planning or take the free advice of salespeople, however well-intentioned, who call themselves estate planners.

There are still substantial tax advantages in the use of a living or testamentary trust. The advantages might not all be of benefit to you, but they still inure to the benefit of your heirs. When we die, each of us is subject to a United States federal estate tax if we have a taxable estate. This is in addition to any state inheritance or estate taxes. In other words, you can pay more than one tax when you die. It is for this reason that you must have proper professional advice in determining your taxes, for an improper analysis can be most costly to your estate.

Any monies we place into a trust for ourselves—such as a living trust—are subject to a tax at our death. Most living trusts are revocable and give income to the trustor. It is for this reason that anything we put into a revocable living trust is taxed to us or against our estate when we die. If we control the trust, we control the assets in the trust. If we can revoke the trust, then we regain control of the assets. This is enough to establish the tax liability. You do not, therefore, save any federal estate taxes on your death by putting assets you own into a revocable living trust. There can, however, be income-tax advantages.

It is possible for the average person who receives proper and competent professional advice to avoid unnecessary estate taxation and certainly to reduce estate taxes to a minimum. For example, in the case of monies or assets you place into a trust for the benefit of a spouse or someone the new tax code identifies as a person being in your own generation, on the death of that person and the termination of the trust, the property can pass to the next generation—perhaps your children—without taxation or probate. This is because your spouse would never have owned the assets and never have had legal title, or what is referred to as "incidence of legal title," as defined in the new tax act. Thus, ownership passes by virtue of *your* death and not the death of the lifetime beneficiary (your spouse). Those trust assets need not be taxed when your spouse dies. However, the tax savings is no longer available to your children at their deaths; that will be a new generation and a different set of tax laws will apply.

A final word concerning the drafting of all trusts: Make sure that you do not tie your spouse's hands so that he or she might lose control of your family. Too many trusts are mere forms, copied by someone who is not interested enough to draft the exact trust to fit your individual needs. These form trusts do not have the flexibility that a beneficiary should enjoy. Many widows complain to me that they haven't seen their children or grandchildren for some years. They explain that their husbands established a trust for their benefit, effective while he was alive, or under his will. When they die, all the assets from the trust automatically go to the children or grandchildren. The children and the grandchildren know this, and they often seem to have less time for grandmother. Consider the consequences of tying your spouse's hands in this way.

It might appall you to know how often I receive such complaints. They are most frequent when a son and/or daughter dies young and the son-in-law or daughter-in-law remarries and allows the grandchildren to grow up remote from the grandparent concerned.

These problems can be avoided if you give your widow or widower the right to include in his or her will the distribution of the trust as he or she sees fit among a selected class of your heirs. This is called *power of appointment*. It means that your widow or widower can, at any time in the future, change his or her will and state: "Under my spouse's trust or under that trust he (or she) established in my behalf, I have the right to give away these assets after my death. I give these assets away in the following manner . . ." I do not recommend that my clients use this power unless they feel that it is absolutely necessary. It involves various tax consequences that are too technical and complicated to explain here. But this simple little device may prevent a widow or widower from ever being lonely.

# 19. POWERS AND DUTIES OF A TRUSTEE AND RIGHTS OF A BENEFICIARY

Many people are afraid of trusts simply because they don't quite understand them. They believe that in establishing a trust they lose control of their property. This is not so. A trustee is a fiduciary; he does not own the trust assets for himself. He owns the trust property for the benefit of the beneficiary. The trustee must not act as the "owner" of assets held in trust. He must act as a "reasonably prudent man," exclusively and solely for the benefit of the beneficiary.

The trust instrument, which is a legal document, should be prepared by your lawyer. Don't allow the trustee bank to prepare the trust for you; this is false economy. It is quite improper for any bank to act as a lawyer and prepare trust instruments, although many banks are guilty of this abuse. They do not protect you quite as much as your own attorney will. They might well give themselves too much power and fail to give you the flexibility you deserve and the rights you should have in your own trust. Have your own attorney prepare the trust instrument—assuming, of course, that he or she is a qualified tax-estate planner, not an ex-colleague recommended by a bank in a retirement community.

Once the trust instrument is prepared and explained to you by your independent attorney, it must be approved by the trustee bank. If the trust is approved, the trustor (you) and the trustee (the bank) both sign the document and it becomes a valid contract. You are protected by the law of contracts, and certain duties and obligations will vest against the trustee. If violation of these duties occurs, you can sue.

When you decide to activate the trust, you deliver the trust assets to the trustee, and these assets are put into the trustee's name as legal owner. The beneficiary—and in most living trusts it is you, the trustor—will retain the equitable ownership. You can clearly see that no one can force a trust upon you. You must sign a trust document in the same manner as you sign any other formal contract.

The creation of a testamentary trust is quite similar. You simply incorporate the formal trust document into your will. You cannot force this trust upon a bank, but assuming that it was prepared by a competent tax-trained estate planner, most banks will accept the trust if there is a reasonable amount of money involved.

The duties, rights, and liabilities of the parties are protected by law. Generally, you can revoke a living trust if you are the trustor, unless you made it irrevocable in the beginning. You can also modify and change the trust. The trustee will usually agree to and accept your change unless it is illegal or most imprudent. The important thing to remember is that the trustee does have the right to refuse your change; if it is refused, you can always revoke the trust and take back all your assets. The trustee has a duty to invest the trust assets in accordance with good business practices. He or she must give all the income it earns to you or spend it for your benefit. He or she must do the same for any beneficiary. The trustee must use all the principal and spend it for your benefit if the income produced is not enough to maintain you. All these things must be spelled out in the trust agreement itself.

I rarely recommend the use of an irrevocable living trust. One exception is that you can prepare a life insurance irrevocable trust and name the trustee or the trust itself as beneficiary. If you name the trust as owner of the policy and live beyond three years from the time you establish and fund the trust, most of the insurance assets that will pass into that trust at your death, for the benefit of your spouse or children, will do so substantially free of death taxes. This is one of the very few ways left to pass assets to your heirs today without excessive estate taxation. Assuming that you live three years beyond the gift, then the premiums you paid the last three years of your life and their pro rata share of the total principal payment is the maximum amount that should be taxed in your estate.

As a result of the severe restrictions placed on passing assets without tax under the 1976 Tax Reform Act, the use of term life insurance as a lifetime gift will probably become increasingly popular. You must be careful when using this vehicle and first seek the advice of competent legal counsel. It is tricky, but it can be done safely with proper professional help. Some of the trust forms offered by a few of the lesser insurance companies as aids to their sales staff in selling term insurance as a tax-avoidance gimmick would appear to be hazardous. Have your own professional adviser prepare any such tax-avoiding trust to fit your particular needs.

In testamentary trusts established under your will, the first beneficiary is usually your spouse. The spouse generally cannot revoke, amend, or alter that trust in any way. It is for this reason that you should first communicate with the beneficiary of your testamentary trust and make sure you understand what his or her needs and wishes are. Allow for these wishes in the trust. The trustee of a testamentary trust has the same duties as the trustee of a living trust. He must hold the assets as a fiduciary for the benefit of a beneficiary and perform in a similar manner. He pays the income to and uses the principal for the benefit of the beneficiary.

Trustees can sell, lease, mortgage, borrow money, and incur expenses like any normal human being or corporation. A trustee's prime duty, of course, is to make the trust property productive. The trustee must preserve the value of this trust asset. He must use reasonable care and skill to develop the maximum income from these assets consistent with conservative, prudent investments that are calculated to have a minimum risk. Most trustees are prevented by law from reckless speculation. They are bound by what is known as the "prudent investor rule," which originates from an old lawsuit, *Harvard College* v. *Amory*.

More than one form of investment is open to trustees. They can purchase bonds, a select list of corporate stocks, real estate, certain first mortgages, and also invest in their so-called common trust funds; these are pooled investments in which you own a proportionate share based on the value of your trust in relation to the total value of the pooled assets. They are not unlike mutual funds. They are, however, better investments than most mutual funds, and cheaper to operate.

A trustee is personally liable to the beneficiaries for any loss or depreciation in the value of the trust that was caused by a breach of trust or imprudent investments. Generally, you need not fear for your trust assets so long as you name the trust department of a full-service bank or a private trust company as trustee. If you name a friend or relative—an individual, that is—as trustee, you may need to start worrying about your trust assets. Under certain circumstances it might be advisable that you name your spouse as a co-trustee of your trust. However, tax problems may result from this, and you must be careful.

I do not intend to imply that financial institutions are insurers of trust monies. If market conditions are such that there is a serious depression, the value of assets in a trust could diminish. These are not insured accounts, such as insured savings accounts. However, if the trustee of your trust is a financial institution and behaves in an imprudent manner or does things with your money that a prudent trustee would not do, then your trustee is liable and you can sue financial institutions. Most financial institutions have bonds posted with the state corporation commission or licensing authority. If your trustee abuses trust assets and invests in imprudent investments, financial institutions have assets that can be reached by an aggrieved party. This is why I do not generally recommend the use of an individual as trustee. Most individuals, if they abuse your trust, do not have sufficient assets to make it worth your while to sue for recovery. A financial institution offers this additional protection. And finally, most competent financial institutions are very careful in the investment of trust monies, and they are certainly experienced.

Trusts pay taxes: They pay income taxes, gift taxes, and real estate taxes. So you can see that a trust is, generally speaking, not strictly a money-saving device.

In many parts of the country there are specialized financial institutions known as *trust companies*. If you are fortunate enough to live in a community where there is a substantial trust company, this is usually one of the best places to bring your trust business. They are, after all, specialists. Unlike most full-service banks, they do not compete with themselves for your money. In other words, in the full-service bank, the commercial section will tell you to put your assets into their (generally poor) investment known as a savings account. The trust department of the same bank will say you should place your assets in their division, setting up a trust. It can all be very confusing to the innocent public. Trust companies concern themselves *only* with proper trust management, so most of them set a minimum amount that they will take into a trust. Unlike some commercial banks, trust companies will not accept small trusts; they want your trust to be economically feasible, practical, and profitable for you as well as for themselves.

# 20.  TRUST ABUSES

For many years I believed that a living trust could be an advantage to almost anyone. Clearly, it offers fantastic advantages to those who need it. Recently, however, since the big push for living trusts, a number of my clients with trusts complain that the monies they pay in annual trust fees amount to substantial sums. This is true. They further complain that the fees are paid out of their income and amount to a large slice of it. This is also true. I reemphasize: The name of the game is money. How can you best maximize your income with the most security? It would be dishonest not to point out that if you don't need a trust—or if the only reason you make a trust is to avoid probate—the money you will pay over the years in annual trust fees, withdrawal fees, and termination fees will usually greatly exceed a probate fee.

Although there is a lot of valid trust business among the retired, there is no reason to sell everyone a trust. However, it would appear that some banks are in the business of selling trusts to every customer, especially in retirement communities. This would be fine if there were a legitimate need and everyone could afford it.

But the need is not universal, and not everyone can afford such a luxury.

Most residents in retirement communities have moved from other states. Without their old sources of information, advice, and other help, they turn to the local banker. In their old community he or she had integrity and kept their personal interests in mind; perhaps he or she was even a lifelong friend. But although the new-business salespeople in the trust departments of those few banks that sell trusts irresponsibly give the impression that they analyze your position and personal needs, they reach the same conclusion every time: You need a trust. Such coincidence is difficult to accept. Add to this the fact that in many retirement communities former trust officers are now leaving the banks to set up private law practices, and through their association with the banks they will often be referred as attorneys by the new-business salespeople who are promoting trusts. These lawyers expect to make a fortune grinding out the same living-trust forms for everyone who comes to their door.

A less than responsible banker always refers you to a lawyer who never questions the banker's motivation, but instead just grinds out trusts. Your needs and costs and similar concerns rarely enter the conversation. You can recognize such a trust officer quite easily. He or she will rarely discuss the costs of a trust with you and will not show much imagination in suggesting lawyers to you, even when there are many lawyers in the retirement community. As a test, you might set up three or four interviews with different banks and trust officers to see if they recommend the same lawyers; if they do, there is perhaps some cause to question their motives. You might well think there is some relationship among these lawyers whom all the banks recommend when there are so many other qualified lawyers in a community of any size.

If you follow the advice of these reckless trust officers, you might wind up with a trust you simply cannot afford. Lawyers who play the game with these trust officers do not work for you; they work for the bank. The bank does not pay them in money (you do!); it pays them in clients and probate fees once you die. Their prime concern would appear to be business *for* the bank in return for business *from* the bank.

Many attorneys are very concerned with trust abuses. If enough retired people who do not need or cannot afford a trust are sold trusts, the whole area of trust law will fall into disrepute. If that happens, a most valuable estate-planning tool will be lost. Many who otherwise could benefit from trusts will become reluctant to use them. It is vital that someone occasionally say, "The emperor isn't wearing any clothes."

# SUMMARY
# OF
# PART FIVE

Two kinds of trusts should concern the retired. The first is a *living trust* (in legal terms, an *inter vivos trust*). The second is a *testamentary trust*. For the purposes of general discussion, the laws relating to both are quite similar. The basic difference is that a living trust is created now, while you live. A testamentary trust is created in your will and is not activated until after your death. A living trust is grounded in contract; thus contract law applies to living trusts. The contract is a simple agreement between you and the trustee. The trustee holds your assets and performs certain services for you; in return you agree to pay a fee.

The drafting of the trust instrument is critical. You should place in the trust instrument itself all necessary rights and commitments. You need proper and correct advice from an independent expert to protect your position. Be suspicious of any trust officer who suggests that the bank will be happy to prepare a trust for you without charge. If you follow such advice, you will pay for the rest of your life. Unfortunately, some trust officers, in their enthusiasm, neglect to go into detail. Have your own lawyer draft the trust instrument. You will then be well protected. If he or she does not do tax-estate planning, have him or her recommend a colleague who does.

Trusts cost money. Make certain you understand the trustee's compensation. Do not create a living trust just to save a probate fee; the money you thus save is a fraction of what you will usually spend for annual trustee's fees. You should regard the fact that a trust will not be probated as an *added* benefit; it should never be the *only* reason for a trust.

There are many valid reasons for creating a living trust, described in the body of this chapter.

The annual fee charged by a trustee is usually a percentage of the entire principal and annual income earned by the trust. Some trust departments charge a fee based solely on the interest or income earned by the trust and do not base their fee on the principal in addition to the income. Make sure you understand the basis of your trustee's fees. If the annual fee is based upon the entire principal plus the earned income, make certain you put only income-producing assets into the trust. For example, it would not be prudent to put your house into the trust and pay a trustee's fee based upon the total value of the house. Unfortunately, many trust departments suggest that you place your house in the trust without a valid reason—other than increasing their fees. Again, check carefully with the trustee. Be certain you understand how and on what the annual fee is based.

Also ask what it will cost you to take anything you put into the trust out of trust. Most withdrawal fees are approximately 1 percent. For this reason, you might begin your trust with only part of your assets, funding it slowly over a year or two. In this manner you can see whether you are happy with the trustee's performance and can live with these trust officers. If not, the cost will be less if you terminate the trust at this time and take your assets back.

If you create a living trust, make it revocable so that you can change or terminate it if you are unhappy with it. There are very few instances in which you should make a living trust for yourself irrevocable. (One exception might be a life insurance trust.) There are, of course, some estate-tax advantages in irrevocable living trusts, but you had better secure proper advice before using that vehicle.

If you have good, secure, quality stocks when you create your trust, don't let the bank sell them and put your assets into their common trust funds. When they sell this stock the trust will have to pay a capital-gains tax, which can be substantial. If your assets are questionable, by all means let the trustee change your investments. One of the valid reasons for a living trust is expert investment advice, but trust departments do have a fondness for their own common trust funds; they cost the banks so little to operate and manage. Make sure you need a common trust fund before you incur the capital-gains tax it may necessitate. If your assets are large enough and good enough, the bank will be happy to keep your trust as a separate trust. You must, however, insist that they do this. Once again, this is the responsibility of the drafter of the instrument and still another reason why you need an independent attorney to draft the trust itself.

The testamentary trust is similar to the living trust. The main difference is that the testamentary trust does not become active until you die. There is no annual trustee's fee until the testamentary trust is activated. If your spouse cannot handle your assets, consider including a testamentary trust in your will. Even if your spouse appears astute and active today, he or she might not be so a few years after you are gone.

If you have a taxable estate (your lawyer or accountant can help you decide if you do), there might be substantial estate-tax savings in the use of a living or testamentary trust. Any estate tax must be paid within a limited time after your death. There are, however, various exclusions, credits, and legal proceedings by which the tax can still be minimized. If your estate is taxable, the death tax might begin at 32 percent. Clearly, the tax is abusive if you don't receive proper professional help to minimize its impact. If you pass ownership of your assets directly to your spouse when you die, there will be a partial tax at your death and a second tax on 100 percent of the assets, when your surviving spouse dies. Since a single person does not have the deductions that are available to a married person, the second death tax is often enormous and way out of proportion. You can save or at least minimize the second death tax when a spouse dies if you use one of the trust vehicles for the benefit of your surviving spouse. A widow or widower is considered a single person and taxed as a single person when he or she dies.

Proper drafting is critical in all trusts. Your spouse cannot change a testamentary trust once you die. Particular care must be taken when you draft the instrument into your will. You should analyze clearly what your spouse will need in order to protect him or her. Your spouse should know what arrangements you are making and must tell you if he or she can live with the terms of the trust. He or she has the same duty to tell you his or her needs here as with the living trust.

In my opinion, no one should ever name anyone or anything as a trustee except the trust department of a full-service bank or a trust company. If you do otherwise there is usually an unhappy beneficiary after your death. Mutual funds are poor trustees. They do not, as a rule, offer valid, full-service trust departments, and their trusts are often impractical and overpriced. It is also possible that you will pay two fees if you have a mutual-fund trust. The mutual fund will probably pay the management company that manages it a fee, as a trustee's fee. And on top of this, they might charge you a second trustee's fee.

Never—absolutely *never*—name your child as your trustee. It is possible that the child will consider this money his or hers before his or her time. The trust department of your full-service bank—and particularly a trust company—are in the business of managing trusts. They understand the nature and the duties of a fiduciary relationship. They have experts analyzing the market constantly. Your child probably has a full-time job and a full-time family. The effort he or she will expend in your behalf may be worthless; it is a serious error to name your child as a trustee. If you have need for a trust, you deserve the services of an expert.

# PART SIX:
## *Probate-Avoidance Tools*

## 21. THE EFFECTS AND DANGERS OF AVOIDING PROBATE

As I have already stated, the *only* way to avoid probate is to own nothing when you die. To do this, you must give away everything you own while you live.

Every probate-avoidance tool requires that you give away what you own while you live—in other words, make someone else the owner of your assets. Those who recommend these tools should instruct you about the legal implications. They should explain the legal and tax effects and the dangers involved. Otherwise, they mislead you.

If you do not understand the meaning of probate-avoidance tools, don't use them. You cannot protect yourself without a thorough understanding of the methods for avoiding probate. When you use any probate-avoidance tool recklessly, there is a strong possibility that you will lose the ownership—and the use—of your assets while you live. Every method used to "avoid" probate has a certain legal consequence as well as a different tax consequence. You should inform yourself before you use them. For example, if you are advised to use joint tenancy, understand that it might delay a probate fee but incur other tax or legal consequences. If your adviser cannot explain these consequences to you, do not follow his or her advice.

Realtors, stockbrokers, mutual-fund salesmen, and clerks at banks are, unfortunately, often uninformed on the legal implications of all probate-avoidance tools, and are simply unqualified to discuss the subject. You will usually be misled when you listen to them or follow their advice. It is the uninformed who adamantly and recklessly push these probate-avoidance tools on everyone. A gullible public, seeking something for nothing, often blindly follows bad advice.

There are three methods by which you can avoid probate. The first is by *outright gift*. You actually give your assets away now, while you live. The second is probably the most popular: *joint tenancy with right of survivorship*. The third, also very popular, is a really abusive form of trust, the two aspects of which are *the savings account in which you name yourself as trustee for someone else* and *the mutual-fund trust*.

Most probate-avoidance tools cause gift taxes to vest immediately: You, the giftor, must pay the tax. And in an alarming number of cases the probate-avoidance tools increase estate taxes once you die. However, the worst abuse is that all probate-avoidance tools greatly restrict your use of your property and in too many instances you lose assets while you live. Let us look at these tools in detail.

## 22. JOINT TENANCY WITH RIGHT OF SURVIVORSHIP

Joint tenancy with right of survivorship is perhaps the best-known method for avoiding probate. But it does not really avoid probate; it only *delays* probate until the survivor dies.

Joint tenancy with right of survivorship is but one of many ways in which you can hold title (ownership) to anything you own. It can be used in real estate, personal property, bank accounts, stocks, bonds, automobiles. There is probably nothing that you cannot own in joint tenancy. You can be a joint owner with two, three, four, or any number of people, corporations, or other legal entities. Anyone who owns anything can hold title to it in joint tenancy with someone else.

Joint tenancy with right of survivorship means that *each* of the joint owners owns everything, or 100 percent of the assets. If you own a house and the title is in your name and the name of your spouse as joint tenants with right of survivorship, each of you owns 100 percent of the house. In other words, each joint tenant does not own 50 percent (or half a house), but you each actually own the entire structure. Therefore, each joint owner has 100 percent interest in the house. If the house is worth $30,000, you don't each have a $15,000 interest. Each of you has a full $30,000 interest in the whole thing. There are, however, other ways to own real estate or personal property in which the different owners can have different percentages of ownership. There are often tax advantages in owning a property other than jointly.

It is because of the 100 percent ownership by each joint tenant that the survivorship feature works. In other words, if each of you owned 100 percent of that house and one of you died, the survivor, having owned 100 percent all along, simply continues to own 100 percent of the house. The same would be true, of course, with common stocks, bank accounts, or anything else. It is this survivorship feature that delays the need for probate when the first joint tenant dies until the last joint tenant dies. For this reason, anything that is owned in joint tenancy with right of survivorship will not be probated at the first death. The deceased joint tenant lost his interest in that property at death. This looks like simplicity itself, does it not? It is. But the simplicity is very expensive—often too costly.

If the deceased joint tenant had a will in which he or she tried to give away his or her ownership interest in that joint property, this part of the will fails. Joint-tenancy assets belong to the surviving joint owner. The house, the car, and the land belong to the surviving joint tenant. Joint-tenancy property cannot be given away by will. At the moment of death, the first joint tenant loses all his or her interest. The surviving joint tenant, having owned 100 percent all along, merely becomes the sole and exclusive owner. This is a very important point. *You cannot give away in your will anything you own as joint tenant with right of survivorship.* Nor can you pass a jointly owned asset on to your children.

This survivorship feature is a two-edged sword. It is probably safe to say that if you put your assets into joint tenancy it would work to your advantage if you became the surviving joint tenant. It is for this reason that one should never use joint tenancy with right of survivorship with anyone except a husband or wife in a first marriage. A husband and wife in a first marriage have the same children, the same heirs. They also would have the same creditors, if any.

When the surviving joint tenant dies, the property will be probated. You will, of course, have delayed probate at the first death, which can be a money-saving feature, though it is not worthwhile except in first marriages. It is impractical to own something jointly with a second spouse in an attempt to save a modest probate fee if that spouse survives you and then owns everything—all your assets along with all of his or her own. This is especially impractical if you want to protect your children by your first marriage. My colleagues and I who practice as estate lawyers can tell you that in the overwhelming majority of cases the surviving spouse in a second or retirement marriage makes a will after the death of the former joint owner in which he or she gives the former joint property away to his or her own children and completely disinherits the children of the now-deceased joint owner. In other words, you might disinherit your children if you use joint tenancy with right of survivorship with a second spouse.

There are other reasons not to use joint tenancy with right of survivorship. It should rarely be used by anyone, even a husband and wife in a first marriage, who has a taxable estate. Serious tax considerations apply. In addition to federal death taxes, there are state death taxes. Taxes are based on the ownership of taxable property. If you die while owning joint assets with your spouse, 50 percent of those assets will be taxed at the first death and 100 percent will be taxed at the second death. That amounts to a 150 percent tax. If you have joint assets with someone other than your spouse, such as a child, the assets are subject to 100 percent tax at the death of *each* joint owner—a 200 percent tax—unless it can be proved that there was no contribution on the part of your deceased joint owner.

If you wish to prove that all the joint property should not be taxed to the estate of the first joint owner to die, you will find that it is possible, but very costly and time-consuming. You must prove to the satisfaction of the Internal Revenue Service that the deceased spouse made no contributions toward the purchase of these assets. Often these records are hard to come by, and legal fees and accounting fees are expensive. Be aware that even if your executor knows enough to claim an exemption from tax, your estate bears the expense and extra burden of proof.

There is still another good reason not to use joint tenancy with right of survivorship. Assume that you are a widow or widower or a single person. If you take something of your own and make another person a joint tenant with you, you may be subject to a gift tax. Take this example: A widow owns 100 shares of AT&T and puts her daughter's name on the stock as a joint tenant. The daughter now owns 100 percent, or 100 shares of AT&T. If she did not pay 100 cents on the dollar for this, then her mother made a gift to her. There can be no other interpretation. A gift tax could vest immediately.

If a gift tax vests and is due, the giftor (the person who makes the gift) must pay the tax. In our example, the mother will have to pay the tax. In some states the tax on savings accounts does not vest until the gift is perfected. Some states rule that the gift vests in savings accounts only when any part of the asset is used by the person who receives the gift (in our example, the daughter) or is perhaps attached by his or her creditors. Other states rule that the moment you make anything joint, it becomes vested, with each joint owner actually owning 50 percent.

It is no longer necessarily worthwhile to make a gift and pay a gift tax, thus reducing your ultimate death or estate tax. The Tax Reform Act of 1976 substantially wiped out any savings along those lines. There can still be an advantage in the intelligent use of gifting programs to children, particularly if you want to prevent future growth of your estate. However, gift taxes and the automatic presumption of gifts in contemplation of death problems are quite tricky, and the layperson would be well advised to seek competent professional advice before using any of these vehicles. Usually, local law in conjunction with federal law will determine if there was a taxable gift, but it is a federal gift tax that must be paid to Uncle Sam.

Today, everyone is subject to the new uniform tax that combines gift and estate taxation. In other words, any gift you make during your lifetime and any estate taxes your estate will pay at your death are combined to give only one limited total of credits from lifetime gift and death tax. It doesn't appear sensible to use and waste your exemptions without proper legal help.

There is still another and even more important reason for not using joint tenancy. Your children are different people, with different obligations. If your child is a joint owner with you, then by definition that child, in the majority of states, owns 100 percent of your assets. If your child has any creditors, you are in trouble, because your child's creditors can take away the joint property. In a growing number of cases, creditors of children who were joint owners with parents have attached and garnisheed the jointly owned property. In other words, they take away your property to pay the debts of your joint owner. I have grieved with many widows over the fact that their bank accounts and savings accounts have been depleted or emptied by their children's creditors. All it takes is one automobile accident. It happens every day. Lawyers and creditors' organizations know that many parents, in an attempt to avoid probate, put the names of their children on things they own. It is naïve to think for a minute that by not telling your child about the joint account or joint stock you make yourself safe. In this age of computers, your child's judgment creditor can check every bank in your community for any account in your name in a few hours, no matter where you live. Whenever a lawyer sues someone for debt, the first question asked is, "Do you have any living parents?" The lawyer then checks through a creditors' organization and runs the computer list of bank accounts in that particular community where mother or father lives. If the parent's name is found and the child's name is also on the bank account, the lawyer then attaches it. It can happen within twenty-four hours. Why take such a risk? Don't use joint tenancy with anyone except a husband or wife in a first marriage, and then only if you have a nontaxable estate.

Joint tenancy with right of survivorship can cost many tax dollars, greatly exceeding a probate fee. Joint tenancy can also cause you to lose your assets while you live. It can further cause you to disinherit your children and family. Because each joint tenant owns all the joint assets, any joint tenant can take them out of the bank and use them as he or she wills. In addition, creditors of each joint tenant can attach joint property.

Never use joint tenancy with second spouses, parents, children, nieces, nephews, or friends. The few areas of practical use and possible savings through the use of joint tenancy are often outweighed by the possible loss of the assets while you live. The benefits of joint tenancy are few; its faults and misuses are many, and the wrong use can be tragic.

In reviewing some of the dangers of joint tenancy, because it is so misused and misunderstood, I have had to oversimplify. Be aware that there are exceptions and more detailed explanations, which you should seek from your own attorney.

The following list of dangers is only partial. If you believe joint tenancy might fit your situation, you should obtain detailed advice from your own lawyer. Be sure he or she has some knowledge of estate planning.

1. In a taxable estate joint tenancy can cause unnecessarily increased federal estate taxes because joint assets are taxed twice—and at a much higher rate the second time.

2. Your joint assets can be used to pay the estate taxes or debts of your joint owner if his or her personal assets are not sufficient and if he or she dies before you.

3. Joint tenancy can cause you unintentionally to disinherit someone. The person you did not intend to inherit your assets sometimes becomes the eventual owner of them. Occasionally I must tell a child that father's or mother's checking account or savings account belongs to a neighbor, whose name was placed on the account by the parent in the belief that the neighbor would pay his or her bills if he or she could not do it. At the parent's death, the account belongs by law to the surviving joint tenant—the neighbor. Thus the parent has disinherited his or her child.

4. Joint tenancy almost always causes gift taxes. In addition, you will waste some of your unified credits from the combined death and gift taxation. If the gift tax is not paid, interest and penalties can vest, which will have to be paid in the future.

There are three important negative factors relating to joint tenancy:

1. Joint tenancy does *not* replace a will.
2. Joint tenancy does *not* save taxes.
3. Joint tenancy does *not* protect *you* while you live.

Generally, it is safe to assume that joint tenancy should only be used in the following circumstances:

1. By a husband and wife with the same heirs
2. When the total assets of both joint tenants are less than the United States federal estate tax credit
3. When assets are placed in joint tenancy slowly over the years, a little at a time, as they are earned

Joint tenancy clearly can be a most expensive mistake. It does not prevent a probate; it merely delays it until the last joint owner dies. The cost of probating the entire assets at the time the last joint owner dies can be much more expensive than two modest probates. In almost every case, estate taxes will be greater than they would have been if you had not used joint tenancy. The alleged advantages of joint tenancy are greatly overrated. Unfortunately, the appearance of such a simple solution can be overwhelmingly appealing. This false simplicity, and failure to explore the meaning of joint tenancy, can cause too many people unnecessary suffering.

Some people make multiple gifts by virtue of putting more than one person's name on their assets. Be very careful. If you put only one child's name on the property to eliminate the problem of a multiple gift tax, you have disinherited your other children, if any. This child has no legal duty subsequent to your death to share these assets with your other children. And often they do not.

The second tax abuse is in the federal estate-tax loss. The federal estate tax, which is the tax on the passing of ownership at your death, is a progressive tax. In other words, the larger the amount of assets, the higher the percentage of tax. When the surviving or last joint tenant dies, everything will be taxed. Everything must therefore be taxed at a higher rate.

Finally, in what is perhaps the worst abuse of joint tenancy, the people who can receive your assets while you live or once you are dead may not be the people you would have chosen. Sometimes these people receive your assets while you live. Let us look at two examples.

A clerk at a savings institution in my community insisted that a woman put her daughter's name on her bank account. The woman told her lawyer that the clerk had insisted that this would save a probate fee, and that the clerk did not agree with the lawyer, who could not convince the woman that this was a dangerous thing to do. She insisted that her daughter did not know about the joint account. She also insisted that her daughter was wealthy and had no need of her mother's money. She was sure that her daughter would never take her money, anyway. The wealthy daughter subsequently went through bankruptcy.

The trustee in this bankruptcy proceedings, fully aware (as all lawyers are) that parents often irresponsibly place their children's names on their own assets, simply asked the bankrupt daughter, "Do you have any living parents?" The daughter said, "Yes; mother," and gave her mother's address. It took the trustee less than two days to have a computer run made on all banks and savings institutions in the mother's community. He found the mother's account with the daughter's name on it. He immediately attached the entire bank account and took the money back East to pay off the daughter's creditors. He wiped the mother out. She sat in her lawyer's office and cried. The lawyer asked her why she had done it when he had begged her not to. Her answer was, "To save a probate fee." The lawyer did not say it aloud, but he thought, "Well then, rejoice. You did, indeed, save a probate fee. You now have nothing to probate."

Another common abuse caused by joint tenancy was suffered by the daughter of a deceased widow who had owned everything in joint tenancy with her husband. His estate was not taxable and it was a first marriage, so there was good reason for joint tenancy. It seemed so simple: She owned everything at his death and she thought this was beautiful. In time she remarried. Since it was so simple the first time, she and the new husband agreed to make everything joint in her second marriage. She died first. She had an emotionally disturbed daughter from her first marriage whom she wished to protect under her will. Unfortunately, her will could not give away jointly owned property. The assets belonged to the surviving joint tenant. Her second husband had no interest in this daughter and disappeared with all his deceased wife's money, which was now his. The daughter is now doomed to life in a state institution.

Many people feel that joint tenancy replaces a will. It does not. Oddly enough, there are some lawyers who also say this. It is absurd. *Nothing replaces a will.* You might not have everything you own in joint tenancy, so you will need a will to dispose of the other things. You might be the surviving joint tenant, who owns everything; certainly at that point you will need a will.

Joint tenancy with right of survivorship can be dangerous. Although many people can benefit from its intelligent use, you must carefully decide whether *you* can afford to use it. Get proper advice from a knowledgeable source before you decide whether it is right for you.

If you are one of those people who can use joint tenancy profitably (and there are many), you will delay a probate fee when the first spouse dies until such time as the surviving spouse dies. There is an advantage to this if it fits your needs and you can use the joint-tenancy vehicle safely. Your attorney will be in a position to analyze this for you.

Should you be a widow or widower and use one child as your joint tenant, you may disinherit your other children, if any. At your death, your surviving joint tenant will own everything and have no duties or obligations to turn any of these assets over to your other children.

Many people put a child's name on their bank accounts or other assets as joint tenants so that in case of illness this child can assist them, maintain them, and pay their bills. This is a human and understandable motive. It is nevertheless very dangerous.

There is a simple and much safer way to obtain the

same protections. You can give power of attorney to any of your children. In this manner, you can keep your assets in your name alone. With the power of attorney, your attorney-in-fact (your child) can still reach all your assets in an emergency. He or she can also maintain you with your money through the use of the power of attorney. Powers of attorney are explained in detail in Part Seven.

Finally, many people don't consider what will happen to their bank accounts if their joint owner dies first. If you live in a state that locks bank accounts (and most states do), your checking account, your savings account, and your time certificates of deposit will be frozen when your joint owner dies.

The great majority of my retired clients unintentionally place their assets in jeopardy through the use of joint tenancy. The public is simply unaware of the tremendous dangers in the use of joint tenancy. No parent, in my opinion, under any circumstances whatsoever, should ever have the name of a child on a savings account, a savings certificate, a checking account, a stock certificate, or a home. The few dollars you might possibly save your estate as the result of alleged probate savings are insignificant compared with the enormous dangers, gift taxation, increased estate taxation, and possible loss you might suffer while you live.

# 23. THE PSEUDO-TRUST THAT IS NOT A TRUST

Part Five, on trusts, illustrated how a valid trust with a trust company or full-service bank as trustee might offer substantial advantages to those who can afford such a luxury and have such a need. Such a trust would eliminate the requirement of a probate since you would give your assets away to the trustee during your lifetime. The valid trust vehicle serves a most useful and practical purpose. However, trusts have been sorely abused by some financial institutions, stockbrokers, and mutual funds. Today, they may recommend that you purchase equities or real estate or place your money in a financial institution's savings account in what looks like a trust but in fact is not.

You can open a savings account in most financial institutions in your name, as trustee for another person. Many people open such savings accounts in their names as trustee for their spouses. The spouses return the favor. Both spouses open similar trust-type accounts in their joint names as trustees for their children and other members of the family. Such an account will usually read (using myself as an example): "Melvin Jay Swartz, Trustee for Beth Ames Swartz (my

*179*

wife)." Mutual funds and stockbrokers sell their wares in a similar manner. This is very dangerous.

If you recall Part Five, you will remember that what you say in a real trust is essentially, "I no longer am the owner of this asset. I make a gift for the benefit of the beneficiary. I give this asset away to the trustee to hold for the benefit of the beneficiary."

What you did, of course, was to give the account away during your lifetime. The same is true with most trust savings accounts. In effect, you say, "I make a gift of this savings account to the beneficiary, and I only hold empty legal title for the benefit of the beneficiary." The beneficiary is therefore the owner of the important equitable title in most instances. (Some states claim that this is not correct, for the gift has never been completed by a delivery of the asset until the death of the trustor.)

Generally, when you hold something as trustee for someone, it is not probated into your estate nor is it available to be used to pay your estate obligations. This is understandable, since you declared yourself to be a trustee.

However, this is not quite a true trust. It lacks almost all the essential elements of a real trust. The trustee has none of the usual duties of a trustee and performs no services for the benefit of the beneficiary. Indeed, the beneficiary usually cannot reach the assets while the trustee lives. The trustee and the trustor, in this instance, are often the same person. This would appear to be a good, secure arrangement. Most financial institutions state that it is a safety feature for you, and use it as a selling point. It is exactly the opposite.

If you, the alleged trustee, become ill, have a stroke, or are otherwise incapacitated so that you cannot go to the bank or financial institution yourself and draw out the money in person, a serious question arises as to who *can* reach that money. Since the alleged beneficiary of the account, usually your child, cannot touch the money until you die, you get no help there. If you become so ill that you need to have a custodian or guardian appointed to take care of you, in many jurisdictions it is highly unlikely that the guardian could reach the money. Your guardian or custodian only has the right to take over what you own.

Different states have different laws relating to this type of account, and it is confusing and expensive to fight your way through any problems that might result. A number of states don't allow them at all. Costly lawsuits requiring court interpretations often result when you use these accounts and their ownership is disputed. Such lawsuits must, by their very nature, be expensive.

If you are retired and cannot reach your savings or other assets because you have them in these trust-type accounts, you could be in a most compromised position. Wouldn't it be ghastly to have a stroke and find yourself residing in a state institution because you had given your money away through a bank account and could not now support yourself? That account will be useless to you if the money cannot be reached while you are alive. The retired are at an age where such things can happen to them. You must be careful to keep assets in your own name alone. There is no reason to place the name of anyone else on your assets, and it is highly dangerous to open a savings account or purchase a time certificate of deposit or a stock certificate in your name as trustee for anyone else.

Such savings accounts are not truly trusts. They are attempts on the part of financial institutions to make you think there is insurance for additional savings accounts so that they can obtain more of your money on deposit. Such accounts are backfiring all over the country. You may buy expensive lawsuits if you thus deposit your savings. The same thing may happen if you purchase stocks in your name as trustee for someone else.

# 24.  THE ABUSIVE TRUST

A few years ago a mutual-fund salesman wrote a book attacking the legal system. Among other things, he attempted to tell you how to avoid a terrible thing called probate. That book stated that you can avoid probate by buying the author's mutual funds, and take title (ownership) either as joint tenant with right of survivorship or in some of his mutual-fund "trusts." Finally, it stated that you can name yourself "trustee" when you purchase a fund sold by the author.

There was nothing new in that information, but you should accept technical legal advice only from your personal attorney, who can give you information for your individual needs.

Mutual-fund companies were impressed with the success of that book—and the monies made by the author-salesman from the subsequent sales of his mutual funds. As a result, today you can purchase any mutual fund in what the fund calls a "trust." You can purchase these funds in your name as trustee or name the fund itself as trustee.

Mutual-fund "trusts" are quite unlike a valid trust with a full-service trust department of a good bank or a trust company as your trustee. These funds provide you with enormously dangerous trust forms without charge. Once again, the appeals of false simplicity and getting something for nothing are overwhelming. People are not told of the 8 percent commissions charged by the funds and many other hazards. Too many of them fall into a dreadful trap. The so-called trust forms provided by the mutual funds do not include any of the services that you would want and get from a valid trust. It is also possible that a mutual fund will take a trustee's fee. This will mean a trust with double fees, since most funds pay a substantial management fee to the company that manages and handles the investment for the mutual-fund company.

A number of my widowed clients are locked into a vicious mutual-fund trust established by their late husbands. These men purchased the fund and named the fund itself as trustee for themselves and their wives. Now that the husbands are dead the trusts are irrevocable. The mutual-fund organization, as trustee, owns all the assets, albeit for the benefit of the now grieving widows.

The rather dismal performance of most mutual funds over the past few years is no longer news. Many of these funds do not provide sufficient income to give the beneficiaries a reasonable standard of living, and most of the trust forms do not allow for an invasion of principal on the demand of the beneficiary. These beneficiaries are therefore stuck with a minimum income. Should they become ill, the boiler-plate, poorly drafted forms provided free of charge by the mutual fund's sales organizations do not allow a trust officer to pay bills and maintain the beneficiaries. These are vital services that any reasonable, ethical trust company or trust department of a full-service bank will provide.

The public has only slowly become aware of the disaster called a "mutual-fund trust." A few such funds now worry about misleading the public. Finally! These few have amended their rigid forms and now allow for some invasion of principal in their canned trust instruments. But have you ever tried to contact a trust officer who lives 1,500 or 2,000 miles away? Even those funds which allegedly allow an invasion of principal rarely provide a trust administrator to handle your account.

Your widow or widower will be most fortunate if she or he can even find the alleged trust officer "in charge" of the account. These fund organizations, however "inadvertently," make it extremely difficult for your widow or widower to reach them by long distance to invade principal to get back some of the money you placed into these "trusts." Remember that the helpful, friendly, efficient salesperson was working for a commission. Once you are dead, he or she is no longer interested in helping your spouse. He or she has no contact with the mutual-fund organization apart from selling. You must make contact directly with the main office of the mutual fund, which is why it is so difficult to receive proper satisfaction from mutual-fund trusts.

Mutual funds, as investment organizations or as trustees, are subject to minimal controls. It is possible that the underworld could purchase that fund and bleed it dry. On the other hand, the private trust institution or the trust department of your full-service bank is constantly checked and audited by state and federal governments. Once again, if your trust officer is in the community where you reside, you can go to his or her office, bang on the desk, and demand either explanations or money. You cannot do this with a mutual-fund office thousands of miles away.

In my opinion, few mutual funds are competent trustees. If you want a trust, don't take shortcuts. Pay the money for proper legal services. Your attorney will prepare a valid trust instrument with invasion rights and many other advantages and benefits at a local full-service bank with a good trust department or at a trust company. It does you and your spouse very little good to "avoid" probate if you lose the use of your assets while either of you lives, and the so-called mutual-fund trust is not anything like a living trust at an appropriate financial institution.

## 25.  THE
WORST TRUST
OF ALL

Occasionally a client walks into my office and asks me to assist in putting everything he or she owns into his or her own name as trustee with himself or herself as beneficiary. This is almost universally an invitation to expensive tax litigation; it can be an invitation to disaster.

There are those who believe that technically you do not have a trust if you are both trustee and beneficiary. A valid trust requires that the equitable title and the legal title be split. You will recall that the trustee owns the empty *legal* title and holds the assets in trust for the benefit of the beneficiary—a different person who has the *equitable* title. If you hold both the equitable and the legal titles, then you own the assets in every respect, regardless of whether or not you call yourself trustee. This can remove the normal trust advantages and cause a loss of tax savings if you make the slightest error in your record-keeping.

It is obvious that when an individual requests this, he or she usually wants to avoid probate and is embarrassed to say so. Recently, one married woman came into my office for assistance. She had an inadequate form which she pulled out of an inaccurate book which had sold very well a few years ago. The form purported to establish a trust wherein she would be trustee for herself. She wanted me to help her complete the form. I refused.

She wanted, in effect, to make herself trustee of everything and name her son as beneficiary. She was married, and had deeds from her husband turning all property over to her. The deeds were improperly executed. They were taken from that same inadequate, poorly drafted book. I asked her what would happen to her husband if she died first. She assumed that her son would take care of her husband—a very irresponsible assumption.

I asked this woman what would happen if her son died shortly after she did. She didn't know, but I said that the son probably had a will giving everything to his wife. How would you like to be living in a home you purchased and paid for and learn only after the fact that it was now owned by your daughter-in-law, who tells you to leave?

So I refused to assist this woman. She went elsewhere for help. I believe she did what she wanted to do, for she was determined to save the probate fee. The fact that she cut off her husband, perhaps causing him to land in a state institution if she should die first, apparently didn't concern her, or was beyond her understanding.

It is the rare person indeed who can receive an advantage by naming himself or herself trustee of his or her own assets without expert help. Do not take your assets and make yourself trustee for your children and cut off your spouse. Even if you are a widow or a widower, do not put your assets in your name as trustee for your children. If you insist on naming yourself trustee of your own trust wherein you are the first beneficiary and your children are the second beneficiaries, then at least protect yourself. Do not name your children as second or "alternate" trustees. It would not do to have yourself declared incompetent so that your children could become trustees. Play safe and at least name a full-service trust department of a full-service bank or a trust company as your alternate trustee if you insist on using this self-trust.

Just as I was reviewing the final portion of this Part, a man walked into my office. He introduced himself and handed me two trust forms. One was drawn by a local title company, the other by a local bank. Both forms predated the 1969 and 1976 tax law changes relating to trusts. He told me he wanted a trust; he asked that I help him fill out these forms. He said it shouldn't cost much money.

I tried to explain to him that his forms no longer applied because of subsequent tax changes. He would not listen, but stated that he didn't want the trust to take effect until after he died. I told him that what he wanted was a testamentary trust, which belongs in a will. His trust forms were suggested forms for a living trust and could not accomplish what he wanted. He glared at me.

Finally, I pulled out a series of suggested trust forms prepared by local banks. Every full-service bank provides suggested trust forms that may be used by an expert to apply to the specific needs of the individual. I tried to tell him that all these forms were different, that they all have different applications and tend to give too much power to the bank. Only an expert can use them properly.

He jumped up, glared at me again, and said furiously, "I have been a real estate man in this community for thirty-five years. Every time I had a lawyer involved in a deal, he blew it!" With this, he walked out.

No doubt such a man, who only wants something for nothing, will fill in the forms himself. It is too bad he will not be around to see the disaster his family will likely suffer.

Since I first wrote *Don't Die Broke!* a number of states have passed laws that allow people to open savings accounts or purchase time certificates of deposit at financial institutions, which would read something to the effect of "Melvin Jay Swartz, POD (Paid on Death) Julianne and Jonathan Swartz (my children)." If I opened such an account, it would mean that I own this account in all aspects alone. Thus, it is being touted as much safer than joint tenancy with right of survivorship. It would also mean that at the moment I died this account, or the monies in such an account, will automatically belong to the beneficiaries—in this instance my children.

I had a client who did this. One of my first clients, he was someone I liked very much. Perhaps this is why I became more involved in the problem than I otherwise might have. He was a bit along in years even before he became my client, and in time, he decided to sell his home and liquidate all of his assets and move into a modified nursing home. He then opened savings accounts, purchased time certificates of deposit at financial institutions in the community in which he lived, and placed all of the accounts in his name POD, for his children. He died. He died broke.

His children came to town. Each visited all of the banks and took the money out of his or her account, for the money truly belonged to each child. The children then went home.

A few days later the local mortician telephoned and asked me what he should do with my late client. I said to him, "If a man in your line doesn't know what to do, I'm not at all sure I can help you."

What had happened is that none of the children bothered to visit Dad over at the mortuary when they hustled into town to grab their money. When the mortician telephoned the children, they said, "Speak to Mr. Swartz; he was Dad's lawyer and is Dad's executor." I agreed with both statements, but told the mortician that I did not intend to accept the appointment as executor for there was no estate to administer. My late client died broke. There was now no money to bury him, pay his estate taxes, past illness expenses, or other bills at the nursing home. I did become involved since he was an old friend, and I convinced his children of the prudence of equally paying the necessary sums to clear Dad's bills, bury him, file a federal estate-tax return, and pay the estate tax.

The point I wish to make is some state legislatures do not consider the meaning of some of the ridiculous laws they pass. Many people feel the law would not be there if it weren't a good one, so a reckless public, not wishing to pay for professional advice that doesn't appear necessary, jumps in, uses the legal vehicle, and then perhaps ends up like my late client. These "Pay on Death" accounts are also dangerous if misused, for obvious reasons.

# SUMMARY
# OF
# PART SIX

The only way to avoid probate is to own nothing when you die. It is important to recognize this fact. There is no other way to avoid probate; you must give what you own away while you live.

All the various probate-avoidance tools have different tax consequences and different legal consequences. Play safe. Don't follow the advice of real estate brokers, mutual-fund salespeople, and financial institution employees, who tell you they will save you a probate fee, but usually don't know what they are talking about. Certainly they don't know the full tax dangers and legal complications. You might lose the use of your assets while you live, and that would be a disaster for you. Very few of the retired can afford to lose their assets. Still fewer of them can replace the assets once they are lost.

The bank wants your money. They will attempt to tell you how to save probate so long as you keep your money in their bank. They are not usually concerned with the dangers to you which their methods cause. The same is true of mutual-fund organizations and savings and loan institutions. Don't be naïve; altruism is not their business. If they can help you in passing while getting your money, fine. But their prime motivation is their profit, not necessarily your security. Don't take chances and lose your money when you might need it most.

There are only three basic ways other than a living trust to save a probate fee.

The first is by gift. You can give your assets away right now.

The second is joint tenancy with right of survivorship. There are enormous dangers when you misuse joint tenancy. Joint tenancy always increases your taxable estate. It can cause unnecessary and severe federal estate taxes. You can lose your assets to the creditors of your joint owner. Your joint assets can be used to pay the taxes and expenses of your joint owner if the joint owner dies first. Joint tenancy can also cause you to disinherit a relative unintentionally. You can't give joint assets away by will; they belong to your joint owner. If you make them joint with one child, you may have disinherited all your other heirs. If you make your assets joint with a second spouse, you may well disinherit all your children.

Joint tenancy can cause expensive gift taxes or mislead you into wasting your combined exemption from gift and estate taxation.

Joint tenancy does not replace a will; it does not save taxes; it does not protect you while you live. Most important, joint tenancy does not prevent probate. Joint tenancy merely delays probate until the last surviving joint owner dies. The cost of probating the entire assets when the last joint owner dies can be much more expensive than two modest probates.

A will is the best way to dispose of your assets. If you are a last surviving joint tenant, you own everything. You then need a will to dispose of those assets after your death.

Joint tenancy can *only* be used *safely* by a husband and wife in a first marriage if everything both spouses own does not amount to a taxable estate.

The final way to avoid probate is a trust vehicle. When you put something into a trust you give it away while you live. You make the trustee the legal owner. This can be very sensible if you have a trust at a trust company or a full-service bank with a competent trust department.

Do not buy mutual funds in your name as trustee for anyone else. Do not buy a mutual fund and make the fund your trustee. It does little good for you to save a probate fee if you lose the use of these assets while you live. Mutual-fund trusts are in no sense full-service trusts.

Do not put your bank accounts in your name as trustee for someone else. You might lose the use of them while you live, and you might have to pay gift taxes. Remember, once you retire you must preserve your assets. Finally, if your state laws allow the use of a Paid on Death account and you open POD accounts, you might indeed die broke.

## PART SEVEN:

*Common Problems,
and Advice
to the Retired*

# 26. WHAT TO DO WHEN YOUR SPOUSE DIES

When your spouse dies, you should do *nothing*. Most widows or widowers are in no condition to do anything right away. There is no emergency, and this is not the time to rush around. Make the necessary funeral arrangements and do little else. Within a week or ten days after the funeral, you should have a conference with your attorney and then plan what must be done.

Do not make funeral arrangements alone. If a son or daughter is not available, take a friend along. Unfortunately, some funeral directors use the occasion of grief to sell elaborate trimmings. This is not the time to waste money. A modest, reasonably priced funeral is all any of us needs. It strikes me that we have all been victimized by some of the elaborate religious and funeral trappings relating to death. Most of us appear to prefer simplicity when we die.

At the time that I write this, I have just finished reading an excellent publication entitled "A Manual of Death Education and Simple Burial." It is published by Cello Press, Burnsville, North Carolina 28714. Everyone would benefit from reading such publications.

Many cities throughout the country have societies

that arrange funerals. Often these funeral societies are run by local churches. You need not be a member of any particular faith to join a society. Family memberships cost between $15 and $25 for life. Members are then entitled to a choice of an "expensive," "reasonable," or "moderate" funeral through the society's contract prices. These societies contract with local funeral directors who guarantee reasonable, efficient, competent, and honest services in good taste. Consider investigating your local funeral society.

When you make funeral arrangements for a spouse, you need the gentle, firm guidance of an impartial close friend. Do not subject yourself to the subtle but high-pressure salesmanship of a funeral director. Try to be prudent in your choices and plans. This is not the time for extravagance or unnecessary and elaborate expenditures.

Most states impose a tax when someone dies; these states will flag or seal any bank account or safe-deposit box owned by a newly deceased depositor. You should take precautionary steps. Each spouse should have a separate bank account in his or her own name. (While you both live, you can reach the other's bank account through the use of a simple power of attorney. Most husbands and wives should give each other the power of attorney.)

Many states will open safe-deposit boxes and release bank accounts to a surviving spouse as soon as the contents have been audited. Make arrangements with the manager of the bank to have safe-deposit boxes and accounts audited at your earliest convenience, or as soon as local law will allow. Your attorney will help you do these things quickly. He or she will also help you obtain tax waivers, which are required to release the money.

If your deceased spouse had a proper estate plan, the attorney will take steps to commence the probate, if this is necessary. He or she will help you obtain the release of joint assets if you and your spouse used joint tenancy. Once your affairs are in order, you should continue to seek proper legal advice. Do not take the advice of uninformed children or the advice of your neighbors as it comes over the back fence.

If you are concerned with investments, find a competent investment adviser (someone who does not work on commission). Do not let him or her churn your investments by buying and selling recklessly. No inexperienced person should speculate in the market. High-income-producing, secured investments should be sought and retained. These investments will slowly hedge against inflation. Do not buy mortgages—they destroy liquidity and can be risky. Do not purchase church bonds—you may be embarrassed to convert the bonds of your own church if you need the money.

You would be well advised not to put the names of your children on any of your assets. If your children are reliable and will not abuse you, consider, with your lawyer's advice, whether it would be safe to prepare a power of attorney for your children. This is different than signing a form at the bank which they call a power-of-attorney form for an individual bank account. I am referring to a general power of attorney, which is discussed further on. In most states it is essential that the power of attorney be completed with a delivery to the "attorney-in-fact" (your children). If your lawyer records the power of attorney, this is often considered delivery. Then your lawyer can hold the power of attorney for safekeeping and make it available to your children when and if it is needed. Your lawyer can deliver it for your child to your local bank and mail your child your checks. Your child will then be able to pay your bills from wherever he or she resides, through the use of this power of attorney. In addition, your child would be able to use the power of attorney to sell any of your assets, should this become necessary. Your lawyer can instruct the child about keeping proper records for receipts and disbursements, because your other heirs will be most anxious about how this one child "attorney-in-fact" is handling your affairs.

If you live in a retirement community, do not sell your house too quickly. The trauma of death after a long marriage is an overwhelming experience. The fewer changes you make at this moment, the better. In particular, don't immediately go to live with your children.

Many children are afflicted with a sense of obligation on the death of a parent. The guilt they feel for ignoring their parents in the past overwhelms them. They now insist that the surviving parent come and live with them. Don't do it. This is always a disaster. You will be nothing but a burden to each other, and you will recover from the emotional trauma more rapidly in your own home than any other place. Very few people can successfully withstand both the death of a spouse and their own removal to a different and strange environment. Stay where you are for a while.

In time, if you wish, sell your home and move into a smaller place. But do not rush. If you go to live with children, lease your home. My experience with clients suggests that you will probably eventually return home.

Once your affairs are in order and your will has been checked by your lawyer, try to lead a normal life. It is important that you keep active. Spend time with your friends; above all, do not mope around the house alone. If you are a widow, leave your husband's name in the telephone book or list your telephone in the name of your husband and yourself. If you want it in your name alone, use your initials rather than your first name. There are people who take advantage of widows' listings. If you live alone and without a close neighbor, you might buy a dog; a dog can be wonderful for one who is alone.

When you visit the bank, tellers and clerks will advise you to put your children's names on your various holdings and bank accounts. *Ignore their advice*. Do not put another person's name on your assets. You can well do without gift-tax problems or loss of your assets to your children's creditors.

Many widows and widowers give their assets away. I feel that no one who has less than $150,000 can afford to give his or her principal to offspring to pay their bills. You want to live on your income and preserve your principal. If you deplete your principal with gifts to your children, you will not be able to live on the income. This will force you to use your principal and lower your standard of living. Remember, once you give an asset away, you cannot usually get it back. Don't be too quick to pay the debts of your children while you live. The best thing you can do for your children is to remain independent. You would not wish them to have to support you. Keep your assets, and keep them in your own name.

Some people run to empty a safe-deposit box as soon as a spouse dies. Don't. Even if you *can* do this, because the bank has not had time to flag the box, you will invite trouble. When the Internal Revenue Service audits the box, their auditors check back records to see when it was last entered. They will assume that you took items of value and will demand an accounting. This can be very difficult or, at best, embarrassing for you.

If the estate of your deceased spouse is taxable, you should seek the assistance of a competent professional adviser. The services of such an individual will probably be necessary to help you determine whether estate or inheritance taxes must be paid. If your deceased spouse's estate is not taxable, you will need help to decide if your own estate will be taxed at your death. Death taxes for a single person are usually at a higher rate, thus leading to more tax because there is no marital deduction. A widow or widower would, of course, be considered a single person at death and the single person's tax rate would apply.

If your deceased spouse's estate is not taxable, you still might have to obtain tax waivers in order to change the joint ownership of your residence into your own name. Many states or transfer agents will require tax waivers before they can change stock certificates into your own name. The tax forms might appear simple, but they are often deceptively complicated and there are many hidden dangers. You can unintentionally cause income-tax problems, or suffer unnecessary taxation if the forms are completed improperly. Seek professional assistance to minimize exposing yourself to financial loss later on. It is doubtful you will find peace of mind by following amateur advisers or by indulging in self-help at this traumatic time in your life. Remember that this is an emotional period for you, and you are vulnerable.

Very few people, of any age, seek professional help before making important decisions. The purchase of a house or an investment doesn't happen every day. These are usually major financial transactions. Nevertheless, few of us inquire or ask the important questions. Often we are embarrassed or don't with to appear unknowledgeable or don't wish to offend the alleged integrity of the salesperson. Or we are afraid to spend a modest amount of money for professional help. Too many of us get stuck.

There is certainly nothing wrong in asking questions. It might make sense to write down the different questions you will want answered. You certainly should ask every question you can, even those that might appear silly to you. Take copies of all brochures and materials. Collect all the facts and study this information carefully before making any major purchase. Don't sign contracts you don't understand. Don't make down payments on purchases until you are sure of everything, especially the availability of your mortgage money or your insurance. Be sure that you understand all your expenses, taxes, and assessments if it is a real estate investment. Be sure you can afford the purchase. Don't make a substantial down payment or earnest money deposit. One dollar can be legal consideration for earnest money on any contract.

I'm not sure where the requirement for earnest money came about, but probably it happened after the advent of brokers and was considered something to bind the deal. It is usually part of the consideration of contract, and when you buy a house it is the amount of money they ask you to put down when you enter into the contract or the escrow. This money you put down is usually part of the purchase price. If you should break the contract and refuse to go through with the deal, you lose the earnest money in the average real estate situation. Of course, you are still liable for breach of contract and all the other legal damages, but most people don't go on to sue for breach of contract; they just relist the property and sell it, being satisfied with taking and keeping the earnest money. For this reason, most brokers ask that you put down a substantial—indeed, a very high—earnest money deposit. Of course, the broker's commission comes right off the top of the earnest money.

The reason most brokers ask for a substantial earnest money deposit is that you are less likely to back out of the deal if you have a lot invested in earnest money. Of course, if you are a widow or widower and selling your family residence, it would probably make sense for you to ask for the highest earnest money deposit available so that you will stop the potential buyer from backing out of your deal. You should know what will be to your best advantage.

Finally, it is essential that you understand all of your rights and duties when you buy or sell anything. If you don't, seek professional help before you sign your name to anything that resembles a contract.

About 7 percent of retired people move to another state, but the vast majority of them stay in the community where they have lived and worked. It is, however, often prudent to consider the advantages of selling your older, larger family residence and purchasing a modest-sized modern garden apartment that will have minimum overhead and minimum repairs. Certainly many widows and widowers no longer require a large home and many of them do sell their homes and move. If you move to another state, a different jurisdiction, there are steps you should take to ensure that your estate will not be subject to loss, double taxation, double probate, and the like at your death.

Some assets cannot usually be taxed by more than one state. Real property (that is, your home) and certain types of personal property can usually be taxed only at their physical location. In other words, the state where these things are located is the state that will tax them. Other assets or personal property can be subject to estate or inheritance taxes in more than one state. Generally, a tax is imposed on the estate of a retiree by the state where he or she was domiciled at the time of death. *Legal domicile* generally means the actual residence and location where the home or apartment is and the intention on the part of the now deceased owner to make that place his or her permanent home. There are many court cases to decide what a legal domicile is. Indeed, there is generally inconsistent treatment in every state about what constitutes a domicile.

There are steps that can be taken to clarify the definition. For example, you might join an organization or affiliate yourself with a religious association in only one state. In addition, you should register your automobile in the state that will be your domicile. You might consider selling your own home before moving to a second home. Register to vote in the state that you choose as your domicile. Change your address on all your brokerage accounts, insurance policies, contracts, trust agreements, and such. You might apply for a United States passport, using your intended residence as your domicile. Redo your will and identify your domicile in your will. Have one safe-deposit box in the state that will be your domicile. File a written declaration at the appropriate courthouse where you wish to be a domiciliary. Finally, be physically present most of the time in the state that is your main domicile. Once estates are in administration, taxing authorities look to the aforementioned items as clues to whether they can tax. Your income can be taxed in more than one state. For this reason, it might become important to determine carefully the place of your domicile.

# 27. THE SECOND, OR COMPANIONSHIP MARRIAGE

Almost two decades in a retirement community have convinced me of the value of a second marriage. This does not mean that I think you should dash out and seek a new spouse. However, if good fortune blesses you and you meet a potentially congenial companion, why try to avoid it? In time, especially if you live in a retirement community, you may want to date. But don't allow yourself to become overwhelmed by romance. Be cautious.

If you date someone, the two of you might become serious. This is fine. Spend time together. Get to know each other well. Analyze the character, traits, drinking habits, and financial position of a prospective second spouse. If you do all these things, and each of you feels that a marriage could work, why not seriously consider it?

Discuss your mutual assets, telling each other honestly what you own. Feel free to discuss normal wishes to protect your respective families. Agree on a premarital contract, which is explained in the next chapter. Talk about pooling your incomes, but do not make any of your assets joint in any way whatsoever. Each of you should retain exclusive and sole ownership of your own assets. (By assets I mean house, stocks, bonds, cash, and insurance monies.) This is essential.

Carefully check each other's health. You should each have a thorough physical examination. Talk to each other's physicians for a mutual appraisal of your respective conditions. There is no reason for either of you to face the prospect of becoming a nurse to the other. Make sure your prospective spouse is in reasonably good health.

You should visit each other's children. Do not be embarrassed to discuss the potential marriage with your children. If they love you, they will understand your need for companionship. Most children will immediately worry about your disinheriting them. Don't be shocked; this is natural. You can relieve their fears by telling them that you are going to sign a premarital contract that will protect your assets. Tell them you intend to keep sole and exclusive ownership of your assets and will not put your new spouse's name on anything you own. But don't let them convince you to put *their* names on what you own.

Some children become outraged. They will still fear the loss of your assets, though they may well say that *your* happiness is the main reason for their opposition. They will reaffirm loyalty to their deceased parent. This is sad, but it should not offend you. At this stage of your life, it is time you were a realist. Usually, it is the widow or widower with a former happy marriage who cannot live alone, which is, after all, a tribute to the first spouse. This is why many second marriages take place quickly. If your first marriage was a disaster, you might well not want to marry again. But if you had a long, happy first marriage, you will probably want to marry a second time.

The intended couple must discuss where they will live after marriage. This is especially important if each has a home. If one spouse sells and moves into the house of the other, some protection is necessary. The spouse who owns the house of residence should change his or her will to allow the new spouse lifetime use of the home. This is a simple procedure and any attorney can thus alter your will for you.

If you do change your will to allow your new spouse the use of your house in the event that you die first, be sure to put into the will itself who is to pay what cost of maintenance. For example, who is to pay the annual real estate taxes? Your heirs who own the house, or your surviving second spouse who will reside in the house? Who is to maintain the exterior grounds? Who is to pay for structural repairs? New roofs? All of these things should be considered or you are going to invite a battle royal between your surviving second spouse and your children.

Once a widow remarries, she can lose her deceased husband's Social Security. If you have your own Social Security, you will not lose this by marrying again. If your Social Security depends solely and exclusively on that of your late husband, it might (but does not always) terminate with your new marriage.

In most states a marriage after your will is executed (signed) revokes that old will, as your assets now pertain to your new spouse. In other words, your new spouse will be in a position to inherit from you as if you had died without a will. If your state statute gives a certain percentage to a spouse not mentioned in a will, your new spouse might receive money under that statute. It is for this reason that *each* of you *must* make a new will after your marriage. In the will you should state that this is a second marriage and that you have signed a premarital contract. You should state that for this reason you leave no assets to your new spouse. Once again, this is a simple procedure that any competent estate attorney can handle for you.

It is appalling how often clients come into my office with a new spouse to convert their assets into joint tenancy. In most cases I am successful in preventing such nonsense. Occasionally, a righteously indignant new spouse tells me there is no danger, for they are going to make a will and divide everything between both families. It sounds nice, but it rarely happens.

Only the uninformed will make his or her accounts and assets joint with a second spouse. There are serious gift-tax consequences as well as other considerations. Reread the chapter on joint tenancy and be aware that all risks explained therein apply to the second marriage. Do not use joint tenancy with a new spouse on any of your assets. Keep all your assets in your own name.

Many states are passing laws that give a surviving husband or wife 50 percent of the deceased spouse's assets, if the deceased spouse did not mention the surviving spouse in a will. If you have a will that gives everything to your children and you never change it to mention your new spouse, or even your new marriage, it will be presumed that you died without a will as to your surviving spouse, and that individual will be able to inherit as much as 50 percent of your total assets in many states. I often advise my clients who are contemplating a second marriage, and who take the time to visit with me to discuss it, that prior to the marriage they should enter into a premarital contract defining their rights and their assets; they should each make a new will identifying their new spouse and they should stop by my office and sign this will after the marriage, but before the honeymoon. There are certain important things that should not be ignored in the name of romance, particularly in a late-in-life retirement second marriage. Do not, however, believe that romance does not exist. It does indeed, and that is why I emphasize this point.

Recently a widow of a second marriage came to my office. I remembered her well; she was the one who had been most righteously indignant when I had insisted that her late second husband, my former client, not make his assets joint with her after their marriage. She was the one who had said that they were certainly going to divide everything between both families under their wills. I had reminded both of them at that time that wills can be changed. She would not hear of it. They made their assets joint. Now she was in my office before going to her second husband's funeral. She wanted an emergency codicil, right then, while she waited. She wanted to give everything she owned (which now included all joint property, most of which had belonged to her now deceased second husband) to her own children. In effect, she disinherited the children of her second husband. I prepared such a codicil.

If I hadn't, another attorney would have. She owned the property since she was the surviving joint tenant. It was her right to do with it as she wished. Such inequity happens daily. Don't convert your assets into joint tenancy with a second spouse. If you do, and you die first, you disinherit your children.

Another widow came to my office to tell me that she planned to marry a widower, but that he didn't own anything. He apparently wanted her to put his name on her home and allow him to use her assets, at least for income purposes, if she predeceased him. In addition, he thought it would be a sign of good faith if she would place his name on her bank accounts. I told her that in my opinion if she did any of these things, one could seriously question her competency. I further advised that it would be most imprudent to marry such an individual unless he signed a premarital contract.

Most states give a widow or widower of *any* marriage (first, second, third) the right to inherit part of the deceased spouse's estate, no matter what your will says. In other words, marriage is, among other things, a legal contract. It vests certain rights of inheritance. It goes without saying that if your intended second spouse in a late-in-life companionship marriage will not sign a premarital contract in which he or she waives all these rights to inherit your property, you should give serious thought before entering into such a marriage.

Most second marriages or retirement marriages have been successful. However, if yours does not endure do not automatically choose divorce. If you were a widow from your prior marriage and received Social

Security as a result of your former deceased husband's employment, you will no longer be a widow if you become divorced. But you may be able to obtain an annulment from your present marriage, which is a legal fiction that is in effect says you were never married. Therefore, in the eyes of the law you would now again become the widow of your first husband and you might be able to receive his Social Security payments again as his surviving widow.

## 28. THE PREMARITAL CONTRACT

Where is it written, what scripture says, that at age 60, it is all over? No more romance! No more physical pleasures. No more zest and awareness of the beauty and excitement in life. Sometimes I think the behavior patterns we place upon our parents are outrageous. Age has nothing to do with affairs of the heart. Older people should and do enjoy all of the normal relationships that they have always enjoyed.

People live longer today. It is inevitable that marriage is increasingly popular among the retired. Many of my clients are entering into their second and third marriages in retirement.

Marriage vests legal relationships with rights and duties. All states have laws that allow a widow or widower to ignore the will of a deceased spouse and take a percentage of that person's estate or assets as a surviving spouse. These rights are often called "dower rights," "curtesy rights," and "statutory distribution rights." Regardless of their titles, it means that your widow or widower in your retirement marriage will be in a position to take a portion of your assets. Thus, you might unintentionally, but substantially, disinherit your children, if you are not careful before you enter into a companionship, retirement marriage.

As I have said, it is important for you and your intended spouse to sign a premarital agreement before you marry in order to protect your assets and heirs. When a companionship marriage does not work, and you do not have a premarital contract, there might be some substantial difficulty in protecting your own assets when you dissolve the marriage. For a variety of reasons it is essential that you consider the premarital contract to protect yourself and your family.

The following is one example of a short-form premarital contract. There are many other essential ingredients that will go into any individual contract that must be tailored to fit your needs. Such a contract, signed by a man and woman before their companionship marriage, is the only efficient and practical way to protect children or heirs of your first marriage.

The following form is offered only as an example of what can be done. There are a variety of uses, reasons for, and types of premarital contracts. You should not prepare a premarital contract without competent legal advice. Each party to the contract should have his or her own lawyer check it carefully.

### PREMARITAL CONTRACT

THIS AGREEMENT, dated the——day of——, 19——, by and between——————, a widow, and————, a widower [or a single person or a divorced man], is executed in the County of——————, State of————, and shall be bound and interpreted by the laws of the State of—————,————. [The State where you reside.] This agreement shall apply to all assets of both parties, wherever located, and shall include after-acquired property.

The consideration for this agreement is the mutual promise of marriage between the parties, wherein they both promise to the other to intermarry in the very near future. If the parties do not marry one month from date of this agreement, this agreement shall be null and void.

Each party has heirs by a former marriage, and each party has assets which are the sole and separate property of each party. There will be no community or joint property owned by the parties, since neither will be gainfully employed subsequent to the marriage.

The parties hereto agree as follows:

1. Each has been fully informed as to the other's assets and property.
2. That all of the assets of—————————which are her sole and separate property at the time of the marriage, and any and all accumulations thereon, will remain her sole and separate property.
3. That all of the assets of—————————which are his sole and separate property at the time of the marriage, and any and all accumulations thereon, will remain his sole and separate property.
4. That during the continuation of the marriage and while the parties are living together as man and wife,————————will be the family provider and will adequately support himself (or herself) and his wife (or her husband). Since both parties are now retired, they will pool their joint incomes to be used for their maintenance.
5. Should the parties separate or this marriage terminate other than by the death of one of the parties, neither party will have any claim upon the other for support, alimony, or assistance; nor will either party have the right to claim against the property of the estate of the other in any manner whatsoever.
6. Upon the termination of this marriage by death of either

party, the survivor agrees to make no claim whatsoever against the property of the decedent nor against his or her estate; the survivor hereby waives the right to dower, curtesy, or homestead rights against the estate or assets of the other except insofar as the deceased person has specifically provided for the surviving party by his or her will or by some form of joint or mutual ownership of assets or by insurance or some similar device.

7. Except as either party may intentionally cause his or her assets to pass to the survivor during his or her lifetime, upon his or her death each party agrees to waive and hereby does waive any and all rights and interests or claims by way of inheritance, descent, distribution, family allowance, or use of home or claim of community property in the estate of the other. Each party waives all rights against the assets of the other which may hereafter be acquired by either party from his or her sole and separate property.

8. Each party specifically reserves the right to dispose of his or her own property by Last Will and Testament. Notwithstanding any of the foregoing portions of this agreement, should the survivor of the parties hereto be a beneficiary under the Last Will and Testament of the other, or as a result of insurance or joint ownership or other form of passage of property upon death, the foregoing will not bar the survivor from receiving that which he or she is specifically authorized to receive.

9. It is anticipated that the parties to this marriage will file a joint income-tax return. This is in no way to be interpreted as making the assets of the parties to this marriage joint.

10. Should the parties, once married, elect to file a joint income-tax return, it shall not be considered in any way an attempt to combine or comingle their assets.

11. Both parties to this agreement state that nothing contained herein shall be considered as a waiver of release of any rights that the surviving spouse may have to Social Security benefits under the Federal Insurance Contribu-

tion Act, and a waiver of any interest in the property of a surviving spouse as herein contained shall not in any way be considered as applying to such Social Security benefits.

This agreement is made in contemplation of marriage with the knowledge that a confidential relationship between husband and wife, and a prospective husband and prospective wife, requires utmost good faith and a high degree of fairness. It is thusly the parties hereto enter into the Prenuptial Agreement, not acting under fraud, duress, or undue influence.

IN WITNESS WHEREOF, the parties hereto have signed this instrument at the place and date first above written.

_____

(signature)

_____

(signature)

To be valid, this agreement must be signed before a notary public by each of you.

# 29. POWER OF ATTORNEY

Many retired husbands and wives should give each other a power of attorney while they are both healthy. In a first marriage, it is a cheap, efficient, practical, safe, and prudent vehicle.

It works this way. If you give a power of attorney to your spouse, this makes your spouse your "attorney-in-fact." With a general power of attorney, you authorize your spouse to reach any of your assets and sign your name on legal documents if for any reason you cannot do so.

Many illnesses plague the retired: You might be unable to sign your name; you might not be able to talk, as the result of a stroke; or you might not be able to walk over to the bank and take out your own money. All these things can be done for you through a power of attorney, which can save enormous sums of money and the trauma of court guardianship or conservatorship. It is unsafe and imprudent to give a power of attorney to a stranger or a friend. Any lawyer can prepare a power of attorney for you. It is a very inexpensive legal document.

Once again, this form is offered only as an example. There is a variety of forms and they should only be

prepared by an attorney to fit your specific needs.
A power of attorney will often read as follows:

## POWER OF ATTORNEY

I, the undersigned, do by these presents, make, constitute
and appoint————————as my true and lawful attorney.
Said attorney shall collect and receive all sums of money,
debts, interest, insurance proceeds, dividends, and annuities
whatsoever, as are now or may hereafter become due, owing,
or payable to me; said attorney shall take all lawful means, in
my name or otherwise, for the recovery of the same. My
attorney shall furthur execute, in my name, receipts, releases,
and satisfactions of every kind; I further authorize my attorney
to enter into my safe-deposit box, located at————————,and
to sell my real estate or sign all deeds, mortgages, releases,
agreements, escrow instructions, notes, contracts, convey-
ances, and orders with regard to said real estate. My attorney-
in-fact is further authorized to sell, negotiate, or transfer any of
my securities, equities, bonds, or Treasury obligations.

My attorney can write checks or withdraw any monies from
savings accounts or time certificates of deposit on my behalf.

My attorney shall be entitled to do all of the aforementioned
in my name as I might or could do if personally present, and I
hereby ratify and confirm all that my said attorney shall lawfully
do or cause to be done by virtue of these presents.

IN WITNESS WHEREOF, I have hereunto set my hand, this
————day of————, 19——.

_____

(your signature)

_____

(your name typewritten)

In some states you can have a *durable power of attorney*, which means that the power of attorney will not

become invalid if you become incompetent. Thus you save the expense of court conservatorships. If you live in such a state, the following paragraph should be inserted before the "IN WITNESS" clause:

> This power of attorney shall not become void due to the imcompetency of the grantor.

This short-form power of attorney should be notarized and signed by you before a notary public. It will be enough to protect you, and can be used no matter where you live. You can revoke your power of attorney while you live and are competent. In most states, incompetency and death will automatically terminate a power of attorney.

There is a variety in the types of powers of attorney. There is a *special* or *limited power of attorney* which you can give someone to do a specific thing. For example, if you move to another state and do not want to bear the expense of going back and forth to your old state just to sell your home, you can give a child that lives in the state a special power of attorney to sell your home upon a certain set of facts and conditions and terms. Powers of attorney should not be used recklessly and should not be prepared by anyone except your own attorney.

The power of attorney form presented here is only one of many different types. It is offered as a guide to enable you to understand your attorney's explanation better. It is not my desire to suggest that you prepare any legal document yourself. They can be tricky and can cause expensive problems, and should be prepared by your personal attorney.

# 30.  SOCIAL SECURITY AND THE RETIRED

Social Security offices in every community are staffed with competent personnel who are agreeable and happy to assist you with any problems without charge. For this reason, a complete analysis of Social Security here is unnecessary. There are also many excellent publications available that explain in simple terms all the average person will have to know about Social Security. Most libraries should have a list of these books.

There are, however, some common problems that seem to affect many people. Such problems relate to the amount of money you are to receive, the amount of your contribution, and the total amount of work periods necessary to qualify you for Social Security.

Social Security payments depend upon your having worked a minimum number of working quarters in an area of employment that is covered by Social Security and that will then earn you "work credits." You may also qualify if you are the spouse, child, or dependent parent of one who earned those "work credits," and who has died before qualifying for retirement Social Security; in such cases you are entitled to receive the Social Security payments of the deceased. Some work is not covered by Social Security; for example, federal, state, or local government jobs, railroad work, and some nonprofit corporations or organizations. If you are not covered on your job by Social Security, you will usually have some other type of similar benefit that is uniquely related to your work. The vast majority of employees are covered by Social Security and thus have some accumulated "work credits."

If you are retired but have not worked enough work quarters and thus did not earn enough "work credits" to receive Social Security payments, it might take very few work quarters to earn the rest of the "work credits" you need to qualify for your own Social Security. Many wives would be well-advised to check into their Social Security background to see whether or not a few work quarters might allow them to receive a separate, independent Social Security payment that will not be affected by the husband's—and that husband's Social Security need not be affected by the wife's separate Social Security payment. You need not work at the same type of job as you did before retirement. Any type of employment covered by Social Security will allow you to add to your accumulated quarters and previously accumulated "work credits."

I believe everyone should check his or her Social Security records every five to ten years while they work. Certainly it makes sense to do it a few years before you retire; you can pick up the forms at your local Social Security office. If you disagree with what you are told, now is the time to do something about it. It certainly doesn't make sense to wait until you are already retired and need the money. If you feel there is an error in your records, a variety of appeals and options are available, which you can usually handle yourself. You can request that the agency reconsider their previous decision and change the records to what you feel is correct. You can thereafter request a hearing by an administrative law judge (this is usually a special hearing officer from the Bureau of Hearing and Appeals) who sits as an arbitrator, listens to your appeal, and will render an appellate decision. These individuals are usually conscientious people who do an excellent job and they do listen to your story. They are reasonable people and will often rule in your favor if they see it that way. Finally, you can request a review by the Appeals Council. The council is also an independent body of serious, conscientious people who seem to do a good and impartial job. All of this can be done without cost to you and without lawyers. However, I might not go much beyond the first appeal without some personal legal advice. Finally you can take the matter to law and go to the United States federal courts, but only after you have exhausted the previously mentioned administrative remedies. Once you go to the federal courts, it will cost some money and you will have to hire your own lawyer. The area of Social Security law is a relatively new field in that it was previously ignored. There is now a sufficient number of elderly persons to warrant that the bar address itself to their problems. I feel this area of the law will become one of the important new areas of practice for many lawyers.

There are constant and substantial changes being made in the Social Security law. Every time two congressmen have lunch, they talk about changing the tax and Social Security laws. It is easy to keep aware of changes in the Social Security law by picking up the annual information publications issued on such subjects by the United States Department of Health, Education and Welfare. The pamphlets are located at your local Social Security Administration office.

Employee and employer contributions to Social Security were just increased this year, and Congress is once again considering another change, for it is becoming increasingly clear to these congressmen that many small or marginal businesses cannot tolerate an increasingly abusive tax. It is highly unlikely that a congressman who likes to eat will allow the system to fail completely; however, drastic changes are clearly necessary.

At the time this book is written, you can earn up to $4,000 a year and still receive 100 percent of your Social Security payments. This figure will increase to $6,000 by 1982. There is talk about removing any limitation on the amount you can earn but it is highly unlikely that Congress will go that far. You still must be over age seventy-two before there is no limit on what you can earn. Of course, your contribution to the Social Security system while you work has also gone up and, all things being equal, the average worker earning between $10,000 and $17,000 a year will contribute approximately $11 to $19 per week, which will be deducted from his or her paycheck.

The age requirements for forced retirement are also changing. You cannot be forced into retirement in most work situations today before age seventy. Some pension plans—such as those for pilots or others engaged in hazardous work—have a forced age requirement that can be as early as fifty-five or sixty. If you are covered by one of those plans, you can indeed be forced to retire early. However, you can start another career after retirement. You certainly are not forced to take Social Security at any particular time. On the other hand, the fact that one can now work to the age of seventy does not mean others must. Social Security is still available to those who wish to retire early at ages sixty-two or sixty-five. Many will not have a difficult time deciding when to retire—whether at sixty, sixty-two, sixty-five, or seventy.

There is a variety of important individual considerations that you must take into account in order to make proper decisions about retirement, and it might be necessary to obtain outside professional assistance in making a determination. Certainly the health of your family and your own health must be important considerations. If you have a terribly sick spouse, you might need the company group medical coverage. You might also work longer, so that if it becomes apparent that you will survive your spouse, you will then want to choose 100 percent of your retirement benefits with no carry-over for a spouse. It strikes me as eminently sensible to have a meeting with your CPA, your insurance adviser, your physician, and your investment counselor to give you important data on which you can base an intelligent decision.

The idea of retiring early and not taking Social Security might make sense. If you are young enough, it is possible to enjoy a second career, a step which will give you two retirement plans with two retirement checks. This can be an important consideration in choosing early retirement if you are employed, say, in a government position. Let's say that I am in my early forties and working at such a career. If I inquire at the benefit section of the government and receive a written statement from an officer there telling me that I have reached the maximum level of service years so that I have perfected my plan for retirement and can receive government retirement benefits—I would then consider finding a new job since I am young enough and perhaps skilled enough. I would then work at two different jobs in my lifetime and receive two retirement pensions. I might also perfect the Social Security benefit. Thus, when I do finally retire— that is, stop working as a gainfully employed individual—I would receive two checks from two independent pension plans and a government Social Security check. In my opinion, one of the maximum benefits received in a service career or career in government is that you have the opportunity to work two consecutive careers and qualify for two separate independent retirement plans. Thus, your standard of living need not decrease when you retire, as it does for the majority of the retired.

The standard of living drops when salaries stop, which complicates and increases the trauma of retiring. It is essential that we look beyond company retirement benefits, beyond Social Security, and into our own investment program to prepare additional income for retirement. Very few retirement plans will give the average worker more than half the salary earned at retirement. You must have advanced into the upper managerial level in order to receive sufficient company benefits upon retirement if you expect to maintain your standard of living. The average employee simply will not. Clearly, it is important that something be saved from income for prudent investment, to provide the difference between your income and your retirement benefit once you retire. One must also move cautiously when making investments with potential retirement money or with limited income once already retired. It is seriously distressing to look at the enormous volume of misleading information in the form of all types of publications by unqualified individuals, addressing themselves to the problems of retirement and the solutions to these problems. Many authors cover the entire field of retirement, including investment, law, tax, emotions, gerontological requirements, dietary needs, and so on. Still, few of these authors have professional credentials in all of those fields, and few of them would qualify to give the type of information and advice on which they write. Fewer still would qualify to practice the professions about which they write. It is your duty to yourself and your family to protect yourself and not follow the advice available without looking to the academic and work experience of the author.

Assuming that you have managed to save and invest and maximize your retirement benefits from your company, there is no reason why you should not continue to make an intelligent choice as to whether or not you should retire early and take early Social Security. The basic problem here appears to be the degree of your loss or gain from Social Security benefits at any given age. To receive help in working with these figures, you can visit your local Social Security office, where they will help you compute the benefits you will receive at the younger age and then compute your benefits for the later age. You can see what you will gain in the three years of early Social Security, and decide how many years after the latter age it will take you to receive enough at the larger payment to catch up and equal what you could have already received from early Social Security.

All things being equal, early Social Security can pay off. On the other hand, if you are at the peak of your earning potential, your Social Security benefits might increase. Thus, there would be a distinct advantage to taking Social Security at the later age unless you have a medical reason for early retirement.

Because of the limits on what you can earn while on Social Security for the first decade, it is necessary to coordinate early retirement with early Social Security. Some important considerations about early retirement are the following:

1. Have you been at your present earning level long enough to receive full value from the company pension or profit-sharing plan? Most plans use your last five years' salary to compute your benefits. Check with the director of your company plan to see if you have been at your present salary long enough for it to be used to determine your benefits.

2. Do you or your dependents need the continuing group medical coverage that you often lose with retirement?

3. Does your family need the group life insurance benefits you will lose with retirement? Company policies usually start to decrease in one to three years after your retirement, and level off at about 25 percent of your original coverage.

4. If your spouse is in poor health and has a limited life expectancy, you might work until you know if it would be better for you to take 100 percent of your retirement benefits or to take less, thus leaving a "carry-over" annuity for your spouse should you die first.

The most common problem relates to proving your qualifications for Social Security. These include:

1. Proper proof of your age
2. Proper proof of marriage
3. Proper proof of Social Security contributions throughout your employment

If you don't have any of these records, you should visit your local Social Security office now, even if you cannot qualify for benefits today. Ask for a list of what they will accept in lieu of the missing proof or papers, and make plans to obtain that information while you have time. Don't wait to qualify until after you retire, when you badly need your Social Security.

If you cannot find or replace a birth certificate, there are acceptable alternative methods for establishing your age, among them:

1. An affidavit from friends or relatives who can attest to the fact that they knew your parents and were alive at the time of your birth and were aware of your birth, and that you were born at a certain place on a certain date

2. The birth records of your physician or hospital

3. Baptismal or early school records
4. Registration for military service
5. Driver's license or voter registration records
6. Fraternal or union membership records

Social Security benefits can also be affected by faulty work or earnings records. Everyone should check with his or her Social Security office prior to retirement. Ask someone there to run a check on your Social Security earnings records. If you find an error, immediately commence the necessary corrective procedures.

Proof of marriage can also be a problem. Various Social Security benefits for widows require proof of marriage. The best proof is the marriage certificate. If you don't have it, and cannot replace it with a certified copy, there are, again, alternative proofs. If you are divorced, your divorce decree can be used as proof. Affidavits from friends and relatives who were present at your marriage can be used. Your attorney will assist you in preparing the proper affidavits and securing the certified records.

Important things to remember about Social Security and the retired include the following:

1. You will need birth certificates or adequate birth records.

2. You will need proper marriage records.

3. Don't wait until you retire to check on your basic benefits.

4. You should consider in advance whether to take Social Security at the early age or the later age. There is a point when additional work will not increase your Social Security benefits. You might well inquire of

your Social Security office to see if you have reached this point.

5. Some widows qualify for Social Security benefits as a result of their own work, as well as a result of a deceased husband's Social Security. Such a person cannot receive two benefits, and should make application for the higher. Again, the Social Security investigator who interviews you will help you determine the higher amount. Widows should retain their husband's Social Security records as proof. Some widows and widowers over the age of sixty can still receive some portion of their former spouse's Social Security even if they remarry.

6. Federal employees are not covered by Social Security, but are covered by the United States Civil Service Retirement Act.

7. Railroad workers are protected under the Railroad Retirement Act, which is similar to but not quite the same as Social Security.

8. Military personnel and civilians are covered by different areas of Social Security. Some military personnel who have had two careers may qualify for the military equivalent of Social Security and receive a Social Security payment as a result of their subsequent work. Application should be made for both if you think you qualify.

9. The present maximum death benefit available under Social Security is $255. It can be less. Not everyone is entitled to a death benefit. The death benefit belongs to a surviving spouse. There seems to be some misunderstanding that it must be paid to a funeral director. This is untrue. The surviving spouse is the

one person who can demand and receive the death benefit, regardless of who pays the funeral bill.

In rare cases I have advised clients not to collect Social Security. It is possible that you can waive other benefits that would be much more valuable to you or your heirs than Social Security payments. For example, under the Tax Reform Act of 1976, there is a provision that some think will allow a farmer or the owner of controlling stock in a small family business to receive special tax treatment on death. This is a special use tax that is far cheaper than a death tax to be paid on the fair market value of your closely held business or farm.

The legal requirements to qualify for the lesser tax treatment are technical, complicated, inconsistent, and so confusing that it is highly unlikely many will qualify. Nevertheless, assuming you can qualify, you must be what is vaguely known as actively engaged in the running of the business or the management of the farm, even if you are allegedly retired. You cannot receive Social Security payments if you are fully employed. In other words, if you want your estate to receive the favorable tax treatment, it will be necessary to make a decision once you retire. Either you do not remain actively engaged in running your farm or managing your business so that you can qualify for the Social Security payments, or you waive the Social Security payments and remain technically involved in the running and management of the farm or business so that when you die you can at least pass the first of many tests in attempting to qualify for the favorable, lesser, estate-tax treatment. It would be sensible for you to obtain professional help to determine whether your estate will qualify for the lesser, more favorable tax treatment before you automatically apply for Social Security at your retirement.

Those involved in retirement planning, retirement services, and government agencies seem to have been unaware of the already retired, when making their plans and decisions relating to retired individuals. There is, however, a healthy sign that we, the currently employed, are finally becoming aware of those already retired. It never made sense to pass laws and regulations concerning retirement, pension plans, and the like, without asking those already retired what is bad, or good, or necessary. Surveys are finally being conducted, and in one question asking whether the retired would have preferred to have continued working to age seventy, a substantial number who were retired for more than five years answered affirmatively.

Is early retirement a panacea? Prior to my early retirement, I might ask a number of my friends who have preceded me into retirement whether or not they are happy. I certainly would not ask those who are newly retired. They might still be in a state of shock, or if they are adjusting to retirement quickly, they haven't had sufficient time to use up their savings or lose their assets through imprudent investment or bad advice. I would seek out those who have been retired more than five years and try to avoid some of their mistakes. It might be my decision that working to age seventy appears to benefit everyone. Business will benefit from using the expertise and will recapture some of the fortune spent to educate employees and managers at all levels. It strikes me as sensible to utilize their experience as long as possible and practicable. Perhaps those who tinker with the Social Security laws might allow those retired who work as consultants to industry to receive a partial salary and still retain Social Security benefits. This would encourage industry to use the talents it has trained. It might encourage other employees to retire early, thus helping to relieve the glut on the job market.

One of my clients retired very early. He has a special talent that the company needed and he could have retained his job indefinitely. While analyzing his retirement benefits and the company plans, we were able to compute that he had reached a point in employment where he would receive a substantial amount from the company retirement plan by taking his early retirement. He could then offset any income loss by signing a contract with the company to work as a consultant for a fee that was larger than his original salary. Such creative use of experience and talent should be used by more employees between the ages of sixty and seventy. If you plan to use your experience and be a consultant when you retire, then you will probably take a later Social Security payment but an earlier retirement.

Many do not know that the blind, disabled, and elderly can receive federal financial assistance (not Social Security) without having worked. Supplementary Security Income for the aged, blind, and disabled (known as SSI) is a federal program, administered through the Social Security office in your community. If you meet any of the requirements and have little or no regular income and very little real estate, stocks, bonds, or jewelry, you might inquire at your local Social Security office. There are strict requirements to receive such help, but in many cases it is available. The same is true with Medicaid. Those who receive SSI will also be eligible for Medicaid, which is supposed to do what Medicare does for those on Social Security.

# SUMMARY
# OF
# PART SEVEN

When your spouse dies, make necessary funeral arrangements, but don't do it alone; take a relative or
friend with you. At that time you need the gentle, firm
guidance of an impartial close friend. Don't subject
yourself, without help, to the subtle but high-pressure
salesmanship of some funeral directors. Be prudent in
your choices and plans; this is not the time for extravagance or elaborate and unnecessary expenditures.

Most states flag a bank account or safe-deposit box
when an owner dies. If you live in such a state, prepare
now. Each spouse should have a small, separate bank
account in his or her own name for emergency purposes. Most states will open safe-deposit boxes and
release bank accounts to a surviving spouse as soon as
the assets have been inventoried. At your earliest
convenience, therefore, make arrangements with your
local bank for an inventory.

Do not put the names of any children on your assets.
Give your child a power of attorney, record it at your
County Recorder's office and then put the original in a
safe place. Don't give it to your child to hold. Let your

lawyer hold it, and instruct him when and to whom he should release it.

Many children will insist that the new widow or widower live with them. Don't do it without a lot of thought. You may be a burden to each other, and it often turns into a disaster.

The death of a longtime spouse is an overwhelming trauma. Don't add to it by changing your environment too quickly. You will probably recover faster and regain your equilibrium earlier in your own environment with your usual friends. Leave your telephone listing in your and your spouse's name. There are predators who look for widows' listings.

Don't buy anything from door-to-door salespeople. Don't make investment choices or change your assets without competent advice. You probably would do well not to attend any of the so-called investment seminars that are pushed daily in most retirement communities. Work only with competent brokers or investment advisers who come well-recommended.

Reread Part Six on probate-avoidance tools. Pay particular attention to the joint-tenancy section and the various types of "trust" savings accounts offered by banks. They are dangerous and can cause you to lose your assets. Don't put a child's name on anything you own unless you want to lose your independence—and quite possibly your assets.

Check with a tax-trained attorney to see if you must file a federal estate-tax return for your late spouse's assets.

Don't rush into a second marriage. If you meet a potentially good companion, spend time together.

The second or companionship marriage has many wonderful advantages. But enter into it only after serious consideration. Before remarrying, be sure that both you and your intended spouse sign a premarital contract prepared by an attorney. Each of you, however, should show it to your own lawyer before signing it.

Never place your assets into a joint relationship with a new spouse in a late-in-life retirement marriage; there are gift-tax problems. Never use joint tenancy with a second spouse; you will lose control of your assets, and the creditors of a new spouse could claim your assets. Each of you should keep your own assets in your own name. Remember, you cannot give away joint-tenancy assets by will. They belong to your joint owner. If you die first, they will belong to your new spouse. You may well thus disinherit your own children. Use your own attorney; your spouse's attorney might inadvertently neglect to warn you of all dangers to you.

In most states you must redo and re-sign your will after a second marriage. Be careful here. Your old will might be revoked in relation to your new spouse. Once again, check with your own independent counsel.

The second marriage can be a wonderful thing, and usually works well in most retirement communities. When it does not work, consider annulment proceedings rather than divorce. If you can get an annulment, the wife will once again become the widow of her first husband and can often regain her Social Security benefits. She cannot do this if she gets a divorce. There are other advantages to an annulment. Check them carefully with your own lawyer.

Every retired person can benefit from one piece of advice: *Don't try to get something for nothing*. Free advice is often useless; cheap advice often backfires. You cannot afford to lose your assets, but you can stop worrying about your future. Protect yourself, and your future will be secured.

# READING MATERIALS OF SPECIAL INTEREST TO THE RETIRED

The United States Government Research Development and Procurement Activity Department produces selected publications of interest to the public. Many of these publications are free and others are quite inexpensive. A substantial number of them are of great value to the retired. You can write to the Consumer Information Center, Pueblo, Colorado 81009, and ask them to send you their catalogue of selected federal publications entitled "The Consumer Information Catalogue." They will send it to you without charge.

Publications available discuss appliances, automobiles, budget and financing, clothing, fabric and laundering, consumer protection and education, food, diet and nutrition, health, cigarettes and alcohol, housing, buying, financing, home safety, heating and cooling systems, landscaping, gardening and pest control, recreation, travel, and other materials of consumer interest. The 1977 publication has a separate listing for retirement years.

Of particular interest to the retired will be such publications as the following:

1. "Budgeting for the Retired Couple" (10¢) is a booklet that discusses planning a retirement budget; it includes a

cost-of-living comparison for retired couples living in selected cities.

2. "Planning for the Later Years" (35¢) is a comprehensive guide for retirement planning that discusses income, health, maintenance, housing, and some legal problems, along with suggested uses of leisure time.

3. "Consumer Guide for Older People" (free) is a pocket guide on how to protect yourself against common frauds and swindles.

4. "Employment and Volunteer Opportunities for Older People" (free).

5. "Food Guide for Older Folks" (40¢) discusses meal planning, buying, and preparing food to insure adequate nutrition for persons over sixty years of age.

6. "Retirement Housing for Older Adults" (free) lists resources and agencies that assist in locating retirement housing.

7. "Your Social Security" (free).

8. "You, The Law and Retirement" (70¢) explains why and how to see a lawyer when planning retirement; discusses making a will, designating power of attorney, setting up trust funds, etc.

9. "Adult Physical Fitness" (35¢) presents graduated fitness programs for adults who have not exercised regularly in several years.

10. "Hearing Aids" (60¢) offers the results of comparative government brand-name testing and a discussion of the selection, maintenance, and care of hearing aids and causes of hearing loss.

11. "Back To Work After Retirement" (60¢) is a fascinating discussion of specific job opportunities for retirees, with help in preparing a resume, writing a letter of application, being interviewed, plus hints on qualifying for jobs through government and private programs.

12. "How to Cope With Arthritis" (60¢).

13. "Federal Benefits for Veterans and Dependents" (85¢).

 14. "Keeping Records—What to Discard" (free).

There are also a number of pamphlets relating to nursing homes and nursing home care, home maintenance and security, security devices such as smoke detectors and burglar alarms. All are analyzed by government agencies; some of the subtitles and subjects covered are landscaping, gardening and pest control, buying, building, financing, housing, appliances, medicine and drugs, diseases and common ailments, diet, nutrition, food purchasing, and automobiles.